Reviewing the Operation of Small Computer Systems

Reviewing the Operation of Small Computer Systems

THE CHANTICO TECHNICAL MANAGEMENT SERIES

QED® Information Sciences, Inc.
Wellesley, Massachusetts

QED Plaza o P.O. Box 181
Wellesley, MA 02181

Originally published by The Chantico Publishing Company
Port Jefferson, New York

Library of Congress Number 85-60180
International Standard Book Number 0-89435-153-2

Printed in the United States of America

REVIEWING THE OPERATION OF SMALL COMPUTER SYSTEMS

TABLE OF CONTENTS

REVIEWING THE OPERATION OF SMALL COMPUTER SYSTEMS

TABLE OF CONTENTS

TABLE OF FIGURES

TABLE OF FIGURES

REVIEWING THE OPERATION OF SMALL COMPUTER SYSTEMS

SECTION 1

OVERVIEW OF MANUAL

The efficient operation of a small computer system requires management to exercise many of the same principles used on large-scale computers. Although many techniques used to manage large computer systems are not applicable on small computer systems, the basic elements of operation remain the same. This manual will discuss all of the elements involved in the operation of a small computer system. These can be broken into the following elements:

- **System Installation and Implementation.** This involves more than installing and checking the system. Vendor support and service after installation will have a significant impact on the operational success of the system and its continued effectiveness. Protection of the system through proper insurance coverage is also of primary concern.

- **Management and Control Functions.** Once fully operational, the effectiveness of the system will depend largely upon the establishment of standards and policies for its use and maintenance. In addition to the management functions, consideration must be given to environmental controls and their relationship to the structure of the organization.

- **Audit Functions.** The management and control functions are of little consequence unless there exists a strong set of auditing procedures to enforce them.

- **System and Software Evaluation.** In addition to the hardware selected, operating system and application software must be evaluated.

- **Operation Procedures.** The operation of the system and the maintenance of control over that system by management will depend upon the procedures and guidelines established regarding operations control. The control forms used to report problems, incidents, and equipment maintenance are also important.

Also included are comprehensive worksheets and checklists to aid in the evaluation of weak points and possible areas for improvement in the operation.

1.1 MANUAL OBJECTIVES

This manual is a reference guide which reviews the operation of small computer systems. The individual objectives of this manual are:

- To provide an understanding of the physical and functional requirements of small computer systems, including vendor service and insurance coverage.
- To discuss the management and control considerations involved in the interaction of users with the system.
- To describe the approach and testing of auditing procedures for both distributed and stand-alone computer systems.
- To discuss the management considerations in the selection, evaluation, testing, and implementation of software for small computer systems.
- To describe policies, procedures, and forms used in the daily operation of small computer systems.

1.2 MANUAL OUTLINE

This manual covers the operation of small computer systems in six sections as follows:

- **Section 2:**

  Summarizes and outlines the various management considerations that should be discussed, analyzed, decided upon, and handled by those who are assigned to implement the small computer systems operation. Checklists are provided for site and installation planning, system implementation and planning, vendor service, fire protection, and insurance coverage.

- **Section 3:**

  Discusses the various operating management and control considerations that should be planned in advance and handled in a manner appropriate to the size and importance of the facility. Checklists cover management reports, documentation and standards, personnel selection and training, user relationships, and quality assurance functions. Also discussed are the various types of environmental and applications controls and their relationship in centralized and decentralized organizations.

- **Section 4:**

  Presents a detailed, step-by-step procedure for auditing stand-alone small computer sites and distributed processing systems. Sixteen audit and control issues are described, and checklists are provided for each issue discussed. Distributed processing system audit concerns are addressed through checklists of distributed hardware, distributed processing, distributed data, and distributed control. A small computer system audit approach as well as audit testing and audit report writing, are also discussed.

- **Section 5:**

  Summarizes and outlines the management considerations in the selection, evaluation, testing, and implementation of software for small computer systems. Checklists are provided for operating and application software issues such as evaluation and testing, implementation and acceptance, systems maintenance, quality assurance, documentation, and training requirements.

- **Section 6:**

  Discusses policies, procedures, and controls for small computer operations. Checklists are provided for initial planning and the later review of these policies and procedures. Control sheets are also provided for equipment care and problem or incident reports.

SECTION 2

INSTALLATION AND SYSTEM IMPLEMENTATION

SECTION OVERVIEW

Much of the overall functionality and ultimate success of a small computer system will depend upon the planning involved before the system is installed. The actual installation and implementation of the system should be performed only after the following functions have been performed:

- an evaluation of the need for and use of the system has been established;
- a management structure has been established;
- guidelines, policies, and procedures have been established;
- an evaluation of the achievement of maximum productivity improvement objectives has been planned;
- costs and benefit projections have been proposed and accepted;
- the project management for the evaluation and selection of the system has been assigned;
- a computer system, both hardware and software, has been selected;
- an evaluation of the risks involved; and
- a strong control environment has been created.

The work with the vendor on the small computer system is far from complete when the system has been selected, acquired and modified to suit the user requirements. Much of the cost and effort in installing a small computer system involves the steps required to make it fully operational. The amount of the user's dependence upon hardware and software vendor assistance in the installation of the system will vary greatly, and should have been defined in the contract. The following will have been significant in the evaluation of alternative systems and must be kept in mind at the time of installation:

- the extent of installation assistance from the vendors involved;
- the availability of a good, complete set of test data;

- the changes necessary in the operational environment at the installation of the system;
- a clear definition of purchaser and vendor responsibilities; and
- the criteria for accepting delivery of the system.

These considerations have been put into checklist form for convenience in reviewing them, assigning tasks, and ensuring that all areas have been covered. The checklists may be used before planning what will be done or, as the effort proceeds, to assure that all important points have been covered. The checklists are designed to aid in analyzing the adequacy and effectiveness of the plans, preperations, and vendor support, in the implementation and acceptance of both the hardware and the software. The following checklists are included:

Figure 2-1: **Site and Installation Planning**

Figure 2-2: **System Implementation Planning**

Figure 2-3: **Vendor Service**

Figure 2-4: **Fire Protection**

Figure 2-5: **Insurance Coverage**

2.1 SITE AND INSTALLATION PLANNING

Small computer systems make minimal demands on the site resources and the surrounding working environment. Frequently, they can be installed in ordinary office space, or even on the factory floor. A "computer room" may be desirable for control, security, and cleanliness of the area, but it may not be necessary. The operating environment must be analyzed, however, to see if it truly is satisfactory for the system.

The checklist in **Figure 2-1, Site and Installation Planning,** will be helpful in determining if all the critical points for the installation have been considered. Questions may be added if the requirements are tighter. The vendor should provide an installation planning kit, which should contain component dimensions and environmental restrictions, as a minimum. It may also contain site planning graph paper with scaled cut-outs of the units.

Temperature:

Small computers are sometimes thought to be able to operate in almost any environment, but their electronics have definite temperature limitations unless they have been specially designed for extreme temperature and shock conditions. Normally, the temperature should be in the range of 60° to 80° F (16° to 26° C). Since the units are small, they can frequently operate in a normally air-conditioned room. Heat dissipation information should be provided by the vendor to analyze the actual cooling needs. An additional air conditioning unit may be necessary, particularly if there are many people or other equipment in the room.

Humidity:

Most systems have an optimum humidity range of 40% to 80%, so they are best maintained at or near 50% humidity. They may be able to operate at as low as 20%, but that would increase the problems of static electricity, which must be considered when deciding on the floor covering. Electronic equipment is affected at both extremes of the humidity range. The effect of static electricity can be devestating to an operation, causing irregular errors.

Dust and Air Purity:

Air filters and air-conditioning systems will normally ensure satisfactory air purity. Corrosive elements in the air from industrial plants may require additional air treatment. Small computer systems are frequently operated in poor conditions in field installations. Doors may be left open and dust tracked in. The operators will have to do more frequent cleaning in such situations.

Figure 2-1
(Page 1)

SITE AND INSTALLATION PLANNING

No.	Item	Response			
		Yes	No	N/A	Comments
	Site Planning				
1.	Has the small computer hardware configuration been established with: a. processor model and size? b. peripheral equipment? c. ancillary equipment (tables, cabinets, etc.)?				
2.	How many people will use the system?				
3.	How many terminals will be used?				
4.	Will all the terminals be in one room?				
5.	If some terminals are remote, have the communications been planned?				
6.	Will the system be expanded in the near future to handle a larger workload?				
7.	Has the volume of printing been established?				
8.	Have the space requirements for the printer, supplies, and report handling been established?				
9.	Has the manufacturer provided site planning and preparation forms and dimensions?				
10.	Has the work and traffic pattern around the computer been studied to see if it is the best location?				
11.	Have all the users agreed on the site area?				
	Site Design				
12.	Have Building Services provided accurate floor plans?				
13.	Has the position of each system component been determined?				

Figure 2-1
(Page 2)

SITE AND INSTALLATION PLANNING

No.	Item	Response			
		Yes	No	N/A	Comments
	<u>Site Design</u> (Continued)				
14.	Is there sufficient service access space around each component?				
15.	Have the signal and power cable routes been determined?				
16.	Are the cables ordered with the system of sufficient length?				
17.	Have the needs for modems and leased telephone lines been determined?				
18.	Have all communications requirements been ordered?				
19.	Has the need for additional air conditioning been determined?				
20.	Has the need for additional air conditioning been determined?				
21.	Has the need for humidity control been determined?				
22.	Has the possible use of special floor covering been studied?				
23.	Has the need for soundproofing been determined?				
24.	Has the control of access to the equipment been decided?				
25.	Have all access control features been designed and ordered?				
26.	Have locations of all operating personnel been agreed upon?				

SITE AND INSTALLATION PLANNING

No.	Item	Response			
		Yes	No	N/A	Comments
	Site Preparation				
27.	Has necessary construction been accomplished?				
28.	Have all necessary electrical circuits been installed? **No. of Circuits** / **Volts** / **Amps** / **Receptacle** _______ _______ _______ _______ _______ _______ _______ _______ _______ _______ _______ _______ _______ _______ _______ _______				
29.	Has required additional air conditioning been installed?				
30.	Has required humidity control been installed?				
31.	Has required floor covering been installed?				
32.	Has required soundproofing been installed?				
33.	Have the areas been cleaned where the system components are to be located?				
	System Delivery				
34.	Has the vendor confirmed that the site preparations are satisfactory?				
35.	Has the carrier, date, and time of system delivery been arranged?				
36.	Has the moving route through the building been planned for the system components?				
37.	Have necessary reservations been made for moving equipment, personnel, elevators, etc.?				

Noise:

The printers, disk drives and the moving operators of small computer systems may create an unacceptable level of noise in an office. Display terminals and the processor are virtually silent. Steps may be necessary to deaden the sound or to isolate the equipment in a separate room. Drapes and carpets are both helpful.

Figure 2-1 covers the above points and a number of other considerations.

2.2 SYSTEM IMPLEMENTATION PLANNING

The implementation of a small computer system obviously requires much less planning than the implementation of a larger system. All the standard planning functions should be carried out, but on a smaller scale. The small computer system is important to the operation of a local area of the organization. It deserves careful analysis and planning at the appropriate level of detail. Project management and control is required to be sure that the project is accomplished as planned, and within cost.

The functional requirements of the system and the work plan will provide a base for positive management control of the installation. Up-to-date project status reports are required, with completion dates of individual tasks, so that the overall schedule of installation can be modified if necessary. Accurate system development data can be used to pinpoint a realistic equipment delivery date long before a new system is delivered. Also, the data collected and analyzed can be used to provide time and cost estimates for future similar projects.

Data gathered with respect to the total time necessary to complete a set of programs may lead to the important, but often undetected, choice of which applications should be put on-line first. It may then be possible to delay the development of programs not immediately required, rather than eliminate the controls and documentation of an application, at great risk and cost, to meet a shorter implementation timeframe.

A sufficient number of hours of free time should be supplied on a similar computer by the vendor to test the systems applications. This may be supplied by early installation of the equipment without charge, or it may not be offered. This is a matter for negotiation. Much of the training in a conversion is done, not in a classroom, but with actual hands-on experience on available equipment.

If there is a Quality Assurance function in the organization, it should be brought in at the time of planning for the system implementation to ensure that sufficient thought is put into how the quality will be controlled, before the work has started.

Figure 2-2, System Implementation Planning is a checklist that covers the critical supervision areas for project management, standards and procedures, and system conversion and testing.

Figure 2-2
(Page 1)

SYSTEM IMPLEMENTATION PLANNING

No.	Item	Response			
		Yes	No	N/A	Comments
	Project Management				
1.	Has the operation of the small computer system been fully described in a Functional Requirements Definition?				
2.	Have the purposes and objectives of the installation been documented and approved?				
3.	Has the system implementation been:				
	a. divided into defined tasks?				
	b. given a project schedule?				
	c. given a project budget?				
4.	Has responsibility been assigned to a single individual for its successful implementation?				
5.	Has a work plan or schedule of work been developed?				
6.	Has the implementation schedule been discussed with the vendor, with mutual agreement?				
7.	Have realistic performance specifications been developed?				
8.	Has an accepted project control system been implemented?				
9.	Have all the users agreed upon the start and finish dates for the implementation project?				
10.	Has a reporting system been established for the project progress?				
11.	Is the project control method the normal approach for your organization?				
	Standards and Procedures				
12.	Have the standards for the system operation been agreed upon?				
13.	Have any formal procedures for the system operation been agreed upon?				

SYSTEM IMPLEMENTATION PLANNING

No.	Item	Response			
		Yes	No	N/A	Comments
	Standards and Procedures (Continued)				
14.	Have written procedures been established for access to: a. the computer room? b. terminal equipment?				
15.	Have written procedures been established for areas of limited access and traffic near the computer?				
16.	Have building maintenance personnel been made aware of the access and cleaning procedures?				
	System Conversion and Testing				
17.	Have details of the system conversion plan been written and approved?				
18.	Has any required off-site test time been arranged?				
19.	Has technical literature about the system been disseminated to all who are involved?				
20.	Will the Operating System and Systems Generation be tested with the vendor's participation?				
21.	Have plans been made for the conversion of application programs?				
22.	Have plans been made for the conversion of data files?				
23.	Have suitable test programs and test data been run on off-site equipment?				
24.	Are all responsibilities for conversion and testing assigned?				
25.	Are the users prepared to cooperate fully in the system conversion and testing?				
26.	Have training plans been made for all system users?				
27.	Has the Quality Assurance group been brought into the planning of the implementation?				

2.3 VENDOR SERVICE

Vendor service may be critical to the successful operation of a small computer system since there are usually only a few technically-trained personnel available internally to support it. The service may be from the vendor's offices or by means of third-party service agreements. If the installation has been an integrated system, or turnkey, contract, then the service will be expected either from one vendor, or coordinated by one vendor. If it is not, there may be a hardware service agreement, a software service agreement, and internal service responsibilities.

Under any arrangement, it is necessary to systematically administer and maintain a computer system of any size. There are electronic, electrical, mechanical, and procedural problems that may arise. The user should, therefore, take the responsibility of maintaining schedules, procedures, and logs for recording and evaluating all system activity, events, operation, and care. A professional approach will maximize system performance and minimize the number of maintenance calls that will be necessary.

The frequency required for vendor preventive maintenance procedures will depend upon the type of equipment, the usage of the system, and the site environment. Maintenance contracts and schedules should be discussed with the vendor and tailored to fit the requirements, while assuring minimum downtime. The vendor should be consulted on the schedule.

Information should always be readily available near the system on the equipment configuration, physical and electrical layouts, communications system information, and operating application system information. The vendor should be responsible to see that much of this information is supplied, and have the system information in convenient form, such as on microfiche.

Performance reports and trouble logs are an absolute necessity on even the smallest system. They provide the information needed to track problems. They can also aid in measuring the efficiency of a system, using a set standard.

Figure 2-3, Vendor Service, is a checklist that points out the important areas of a vendor service contract, and reviews the responsibility of both the vendor and the user, since both are interested in a successful relationship.

2.4 FIRE PROTECTION

Fire protection planning is a fundamental part of system installation planning. It is occasionally overlooked when the new computer system is to be installed in a general business area or factory, but computers have special considerations which must be handled. First, they are electronic and electrical equipment, with flammable insulation and paper products in and around them. They are susceptible to fire in a unique way. Second, they often contain valuable or important information that cannot be readily reconstructed, so special care should be taken for their protection.

VENDOR SERVICE

No.	Item	Response: Yes	No	N/A	Comments
1.	Do the contract and vendor literature clearly state the responsibilities and guarantees of the vendor in delivering and installing the system?				
2.	If there are contracts for hardware and software from two different vendors, is there mutual agreement between them and acceptance of all conditions?				
3.	Are the vendor representatives who will be supplied for Field Service, Engineering Service, or Account Management, clearly spelled out in the agreements?				
4.	Has a Service Maintenance Agreement been prepared with either the vendor or a third-party service organization?				
5.	Are you satisfied with the guaranteed speed with which maintenance will be accomplished, considering: a. the location of the nearest vendor supply point? b. the availability of temporary or replacement equipment while yours is being repaired? c. the location of an office to which you can take hardware for repair or trade? d. the supply parts that will be left on-site for emergencies?				
6.	Have you agreed with your responsibilities: a. to have adequate operating supplies on-site, including disk cartridges, disk packs, filters, magnetic tape and cassettes, printer ribbons, printer paper, etc.? b. to have adequate accessories, such as storage for disks, tapes, cartridges, etc., and tables, cabinets, and chairs? c. to keep the necessary documentation available in a location convenient to the system?				

VENDOR SERVICE

No.	Item	Response			
		Yes	No	N/A	Comments
6.	(Continued) d. to perform the specific maintenance and care operations required at the suggested frequencies or when necessary? e. to manage the electrical and environmental systems adequately? f. to keep the system exterior and the surrounding area clean?				
7.	Will the vendor supply names of individuals for service or emergencies?				
8.	Will the vendor supply telephone numbers for service or emergency contact on a 7-day week, 24-hour basis?				
9.	Does the vendor maintenance agreement clearly spell out: a. the maintenance charges and possible extra charges? b. the availability of the maintenance service by day and hour? c. the frequency and coverage of routine preventive maintenance? d. exclusions that are the customer's responsibility? e. requirements on vendor access to the system? f. availability of additional equipment or replacement equipment? g. installation and control of engineering and safety changes? h. other services that have been agreed upon? i. vendor rights to assign service agreements to other agents?				
10.	Does the vendor supply adequate details on equipment care by the customer?				

VENDOR SERVICE

No.	Item	Response			
		Yes	No	N/A	Comments
11.	Does the vendor supply a reporting system or forms for: a. daily usage and equipment activity log? b. system configuration changes? c. vendor field service log?				
12.	Is there a useful Problem Reporting Procedure, or Trouble Log, to keep a permanent record of troubles experienced and trouble calls to the vendor?				
13.	Does the vendor supply reasonable system diagnostic software with error printouts and status reports?				
14.	Is there adequate documentation on the recommended preventive maintenance (PM), including: a. PM frequency, schedules, and estimated times? b. recommended PM tools and test equipment? c. information on microfiche relative to the system?				
15.	Have other customers, used as references, commented on areas of the Vendor Service which should be clarified or written in the contract?				
16.	Will adequate Vendor Technical Support be available if problems arise with either your hardware or software systems?				

Many organizations hold internal personnel responsible for fire safety and building construction. These personnel should be consulted during the planning period, and should be informed about both the hazards and the criticality of the operation. The standard organizational fire and emergency procedures should be studied and understood by the computer group, and special training should be given to those closest to the operation.

A small computer system may be in an open operational area or in a special room, but it is seldom placed in a highly-controlled computer room as are the larger computers. There must, however, be no less attention paid to fire protection.

Figure 2-4, Fire Protection, is a checklist that covers the fire protection and fire control preparations that must be considered.

2.5 INSURANCE COVERAGE

Insurance does not prevent or detect security violations, but it can reduce the impact of loss. Insurance should be thought of as a control which may be analyzed and applied before the operation starts. It requires the same thorough evaluation as any other control. The final decision on insurance coverage will be determined by the organization policy on such matters. The decision can best be made if the data processing manager:

- analyzes the value of the systems and information;
- documents the analysis;
- considers the probabilities of security infractions or events;
- considers the probabilities of a disaster striking the operation.

There will be three basic types of insurance policies to discuss:

1. Fire Insurance
2. Valuable Papers and Records Insurance
3. All-Risk Data Processing Insurance, with Media and Records Section

The principle of insurance coverage is to transfer risk of major loss to another organization. Each company or organization will have its own standards as to what risk it will hold internally and what risk is to be transferred.

There will normally be an insurance manager, or equivalent, responsible for deciding the degree of risk to be insured. It is the responsibility of the data processing manager to present the problem to the insurance manager. He should first estimate the possible exposure. He should then outline in detail all the equipment, records, and media under his control, stating their replacement cost and actual cash value.

FIRE PROTECTION

No.	Item	Response			
		Yes	No	N/A	Comments
1.	Have all organizational procedures relative to fire protection and control been reviewed and implemented as appropriate?				
2.	Have the on-site personnel been instructed and equipped to take immediate action against incipient and relatively insignificant fires?				
3.	Have the personnel been instructed in fire reporting procedures and early action?				
4.	Are extinguishers readily available that are appropriate to both electrical and paper fires?				
5.	Is the area protected by a sprinkler system?				
6.	Is there generally good housekeeping around the computer area?				
7.	Are there fire detectors located both in the computer room and the supplies and storage area?				
8.	Are there devices installed for both heat and smoke detection?				
9.	Is there a portable fire extinguisher clearly marked and strategically placed near the computer area?				
10.	Has all construction and wiring been done according to local codes?				
11.	Does the computer room have a Class A fire rating of at least two hours, and do the walls extend from true floor to true ceiling?				
12.	If the computer is not in a computer room, are there adequate fire detection devices, sprinklers, and fire extinguishers in the general area?				
13.	Do safes and vaults that are used carry the Safe Manufacturer's National Association (SMNA) or the Underwriters Laboratories (UL) seal?				

FIRE PROTECTION

No.	Item	Response			
		Yes	No	N/A	Comments
14.	Has emergency battery lighting been provided for the computer area that operates after the main power has been cut off?				
15.	Does a policy of "no smoking" exist in the computer area?				
16.	Are cleaning personnel instructed in the precautions to be exercised around the computer equipment?				
17.	Are there written emergency procedures for fire reporting, fire fighting, and requesting assistance?				
18.	Has a fire survey been made of the area by internal buildings personnel or the local fire department?				
19.	Have all aspects of the survey report been handled adequately?				

The need for this coverage, or any other special insurance coverage, such as third party liability, business interruption, and so on, should be clearly defined. There may be, for example, a considerable business interruption loss which could be insured. This is not normally under the data processing manager's control, however. It should be reviewed and requested by the user management together with the insurance manager.

When data processing equipment is leased or rented, the insurance on it may be borne by the owner. This should be verified in the contract.

The insurance manager will also be concerned that all legal requirements for fire safety are being met in the facility. Insurance will only be valid if there is full compliance with all fire and safety laws. It is wise to request inspections by both the insurance company and the local fire department. Fire department familiarity with your installation is, in itself, a useful precaution. Contingency Plans are also useful.

Insurance analysis procedures and forms are provided in the **FTP Technical Library publication, "EDP Security: Data, Facilities, Personnel, Control." Figure 2-5, Insurance Coverage,** is a checklist for reviewing the principal points to consider during the analysis and preparation effort.

Figure 2-5

INSURANCE COVERAGE

No.	Item	Response			
		Yes	No	N/A	Comments
1.	Has a "vital records" analysis been made of the information involved in the computer system?				
2.	Has the vital records analysis established the dependency on computer records and files?				
3.	Have all vital computer records been identified for backup, safe storage, and insurance consideration?				
4.	Has an assessment been made of the value of the software and systems for insurance purposes?				
5.	Is there a need for employee restrictive agreements regarding the disclosure and release of information, which may indicate a need for insurance coverage?				
6.	When the organization is receiving outside data processing services, are adequate insurance safeguards in place?				
7.	Does the existing property (building and equipment) insurance of the organization include the additional problems that may affect computers, such as air-conditioning breakdown, electrical failure, etc.?				
8.	Have the effects been considered of the computer application systems which could result in computer-related embezzlement, forgery, or loss of trade secrets?				
9.	If poor systems or computer operations result in the complete or partial destruction of valuable files or information, is the loss covered by insurance?				
10.	Does the organization presently have insurance against the loss of "valuable papers" (such as accounts receivable, fixed assets records, etc.) when the information is on computer media?				
11.	Is the organization insured against the dishonest acts of employees, such as the programmers as well as the operators?				
12.	Has insurance of the software written in-house been considered?				

SECTION 3

MANAGEMENT AND CONTROL CONSIDERATIONS

SECTION OVERVIEW

The planning for the organization, staffing, documentation, and reporting systems, control functions, and related staff functions, is one of the keys to a successful and smoothly-operating computer system. The continued success of the operation and its effect on productivity improvement is dependent upon judicious and continuous management. Small computer centers are certainly not as complex as the large, highly-controlled computer centers, but similar management functions must be handled responsibly if the operation is to succeed. The following checklists are provided to assist in establishing these functions:

Figure 3-1: **Operating Organization**

Figure 3-2: **Management Reports**

Figure 3-3: **Documentation and Standards**

Figure 3-4: **Personnel Selection and Training**

Figure 3-5: **User Relationships**

Figure 3-6: **Quality Assurance Functions**

The internal control environment established by management has a significant impact on the selection and effectiveness of an organization's data processing control procedures and techniques. In a decentralized organization, such as in the use of small computer systems, there are fewer environmental controls in place, so much more attention must be paid to the application controls. The astute manager of a small computer system will be able to readily determine where the data processing operation fits into the overall control picture and ensure that suitable guidelines, policies, and procedures are prepared, and plans and performance reviews and measurements are conducted. The following checklists include the level of control in the organizational structure, higher management's responsibilities, as well as the supervision of data processing systems:

Figure 3-8: **Evaluation of Control Atmosphere**

Figure 3-9: **Authorization Environmental Controls**

Figure 3-10: **Recording Environmental Controls**

Figure 3-11: **Assets Safeguarding Environmental Controls**

Figure 3-12: **Accountability Environmental Controls**

Figure 3-13: **Performance Environmental Controls**

Figure 3-14: **Program/Systems Environmental Controls**

3.1 ORGANIZATIONAL MANAGEMENT

The organizational group which operates the small computer system, whether one person or several, should report functionally to the user group for which it is working and should have a specific, written set of responsibilities and objectives. If the organization is set up for good management and responsive operation, the opportunities for achieving productivity improvements can best be realized.

Only a few of the most important considerations are included in the checklist in **Figure 3-1, Operating Organization.** Other problems of organization and management are the same as for any other part of the organization.

- **Management Reports:**

A small computer system is identical in management requirements to a large computer system, although the costs, personnel, and problems tend to be on a much smaller scale. The operation should be managed in the same standard ways that have been proven over many years in the operation of computers. After a responsible organization has been established, there should be sufficient internal controls and adequate reporting of the operation and control of the system.

The checklist in **Figure 3-2, Management Reports,** mentions the key management reports which should be in place.

- **Documentation and Standards:**

Documentation of both operations and applications must be systematic, controlled, and adequate. Special attention should be paid to it because it is often given low priority in small groups where "everyone knows the system." When troubles occur, or when key individuals are unavailable, they realize how little they know about the system. Standards increase productivity by reducing complexity and making the elements of systems familiar to all. Documentation increases productivity, by having correct, detailed information available when it is needed for management, control, trouble-shooting, and systems analysis.

The checklist in **Figure 3-3, Documentation and Standards,** indicates the documentation elements and standards which are most critical to maintain.

OPERATING ORGANIZATION

No.	Item	Response			
		Yes	No	N/A	Comments
1.	Has a manager for the small computer operation, who reports functionally to the user group, been appointed?				
2.	Have the Technical Support personnel in the central organization agreed to specific support of the operation?				
3.	If there are no available Technical Support personnel, have arrangements been made for such support with either the vendor or a third party?				
4.	Does the computer operations group have a written set of responsibilities and objectives?				
5.	Does the computer operations group have authority to reject systems that do not fit the accepted operating considerations?				
6.	Has the authority for personnel selection and management been vested in the computer operations manager, rather than the users, who will use the computer from terminals?				
7.	Is control being exercised to verify the operator's adherence to standard operating procedures by examination of operating logs and review of significant events?				
8.	Are adequate machine operation logs maintained which provide: a. entry of each machine operation exception? b. operator actions taken for exception? c. rerun actions taken?				
9.	Is the use of the system library recorded automatically?				
10.	Are processing and report distribution instructions recorded and reviewed?				
11.	Does the computer operations group operate as an integral part of the organizational group to which it reports?				

Figure 3-2

MANAGEMENT REPORTS

No.	Item	Response			
		Yes	No	N/A	Comments
1.	Are brief operations reports, with exception information, prepared routinely by the computer group?				
2.	Are the following basic operating statistics produced routinely? a. resource utilization? b. problems or incidents? c. daily operations, listing priorities? d. schedule adherence, both users and operations? e. job turnaround time?				
3.	Are Resource Usage Accounting systems being used on the computer, if they are available?				
4.	Are the following cost and personnel reports produced routinely: a. total cost or budget adherence? b. unit costs for jobs run? c. overhead costs for systems and support?				
5.	Are the following performance indicators calculated and reported: a. cost-effectiveness, or resource productivity? b. daily productive time and output? c. actual work volume versus planned work volume? d. work quality, or Quality Assurance reports?				
6.	Do the trouble or incident reports specify the particular trouble conditions for analysis and responsibility?				
7.	Are the trouble or incident reports acted upon and followed up by management?				
8.	Is there a complete inventory list available of all hardware, software, and ancillary equipment?				
9.	Is there an adequate inventory control system of necessary supplies to avoid stockouts?				
10.	Are special forms controlled by an individual, with their use reported to management?				

3.2 PERSONNEL SELECTION AND TRAINING

The selection of the staff involves getting the proper level of commitment from the organization and the individuals selected.

Organizational Commitment:

Top executive levels within the organization should be made aware of the importance of the effort to coordinate and plan the smooth evolution to automated systems. The need to find and staff the effort at the appropriate levels with the right individuals is the first step in the commitment to the effort. Management commitment and support help assure that the individuals selected have a better chance of implementing the changes in an atmosphere of acceptance.

Individual Commitment:

The staff members selected should not only have the proper skills, but must also be dedicated to designing and implementing systems that truly use the available capabilities of the systems.

- **Personnel Selection:**

Three avenues should be considered as sources for staffing small computer operators:

1. **Internal:** Staff can be selected from the existing organization by reviewing the skills, experience, and aptitude of personnel within the data processing or user functions. The key individual within the staff is the manager who will be the "change-agent" for the future.

2. **External:** Recruiting from outside the organization may be feasible, but the job specifications may make it difficult to find and recruit people. Going outside the organization will necessarily entail hiring someone who is not familiar with the organization. Overriding this consideration may be the experience, expertise, and innovation an individual can bring to the project. Knowledge of the organization can be provided through alternative means, such as using other staff members as part of the team.

3. **Consultants:** A large amount of external expertise can be brought in and concentrated within the organization in a short period of time through the use of consultants. They should never be hired before the goals and feasibility have been agreed upon.

Figure 3-3
(Page 1)

DOCUMENTATION AND STANDARDS

No.	Item	Response			
		Yes	No	N/A	Comments
1.	Has the vendor supplied adequate documentation of the hardware and operating systems?				
2.	Does each application system have documentation, including:				
	a. run book adhering to accepted standards?				
	b. systems flowchart?				
	c. list of source, object, and load modules?				
	d. list of disks, tapes, and cassettes with their retention period?				
	e. special operation requirements?				
	f. backup and trouble-shooting procedures?				
	g. file organization description for each data set?				
	h. details of report distribution?				
3.	Are there standards which have been developed and used for:				
	a. system design?				
	b. programming methods and languages?				
	c. operations?				
	d. control?				
	e. documentation?				
4.	Is documentation included in the system installation project control?				
5.	If changes are made to the system, is the documentation updated?				
6.	Are copies of the documentation of operating procedures and systems stored in a safe, secure, place?				
7.	Is there an operations and systems standards manual maintained in the organization?				

Figure 3-3
(Page 2)

DOCUMENTATION AND STANDARDS

No.	Item	Response			
		Yes	No	N/A	Comments
8.	Does the manual define standards for: a. systems design? b. systems descriptions and documentation? c. data structures and files? d. control requirements? e. manual procedures? f. test requirements?				
9.	Are programs required to be written: a. in one of a few selected languages and versions? b. for one or two standard operating systems? c. with approved controls? d. using selected utility programs?				

- **Training:**

To be effective and to increase productivity, training must be timely and appropriate. It must be analyzed and planned in an organized manner. It must never consist of a standard set of courses with a set curriculum that is always followed. Training must be responsive to present or future needs. Only then, when it is presented professionally and enthusiastically, will training supply the necessary motivation to get people to learn and to apply their new knowledge and skills on their jobs.

Appropriate training that is given in a timely fashion is the key to improving both individual and organizational productivity. The checklist included in **Figure 3-4, Personnel Selection and Training,** should be considered, if appropriate to your organization.

3.3 USER RELATIONSHIPS

The small computer system may be completely imbedded in the user organization, but it usually still remains a separate entity that is heavily used but not fully understood by most users. Although both the users and the computer system supervision may report to the same manager, they must also have considerable routine and direct communication. Clear understandings as to the level of service to be expected should be developed. Problems in either direction, or service complaints should be handled informally and rapidly, yet documented and analyzed. Patterns of the problems need to be discussed fully.

The user's feelings about responsiveness may be qualitative, but they are important. They are best met by developing an understanding about performance measures and the reporting of their accomplishment (turnaround time, etc.), so that quantitative data about the level of service may be discussed.

Some key points in smoothing user relationships with a computer operation are included in **Figure 3-5, User Relationships.**

3.4 QUALITY ASSURANCE FUNCTION

Quality Assurance (QA) review has not yet been applied to the majority of data processing systems in operation, but QA has become recognized as an important function for adequate management and control. QA is a function that is needed to assure that each computer project solves the problem it was intended to solve in accordance with the organization's policies and procedures and at a reasonable cost. QA reviews can aid in evaluating an application system's quality throughout its life cycle, in development, installation, operation, and modification. Whether or not there is an assigned QA function in your organization, QA methods may be applied to reviewing any system to see if it meets the users' specified needs under the required control and management.

Figure 3-4
(Page 1)

PERSONNEL SELECTION AND TRAINING

No.	Item	Response			
		Yes	No	N/A	Comments
	Personnel Selection				
1.	Are all personnel positions for the small computer system planned on an organization chart?				
2.	Have position descriptions been written or obtained for the special positions involved in the operation?				
3.	Is there an organizational commitment to selecting capable individuals for the systems operations?				
4.	If there are sufficient positions available, have people with data processing experience and organizational experience both been considered?				
5.	Have possible career paths been described for those who will handle the computer operation?				
6.	Have objectives been established to judge personnel performance and productivity systematically?				
7.	Are the positions described in terms of both organizational objectives and work assignments?				
8.	Has adherence to the laws considering equal employment opportunity and personal privacy been considered?				
9.	Have special experiences in data processing been considered in setting salary levels?				
	Personnel Training				
10.	Have training plans been set up for:				
	a. user management personnel?				
	b. user operational personnel?				
	c. computer operators?				
	d. systems analysts and programmers?				
	e. control and audit personnel?				

PERSONNEL SELECTION AND TRAINING

No.	Item	Response			
		Yes	No	N/A	Comments
	Personnel Training (Continued)				
11.	Have all of the following training methods been considered? a. vendor training classes? b. internal training classes? c. third-party commercial training classes? d. Computer-Assisted Instruction (CAI)? e. technical meetings and seminars? f. hands-on in a central installation?				
12.	If your organization has an internal training group, have training possibilities and plans been discussed?				
13.	Have the basic skills required in the introduction and operation of the systems been analyzed and documented?				
14.	Are the core training efforts directed to the attainment of those basic skills in a necessary group of people?				
15.	Is the training curriculum related to the job descriptions?				
16.	Can users who wish to become more involved with the computer gain free access to the training courses?				
17.	Have the training objectives been discussed with affected user management?				
18.	Has responsibility for training been specifically assigned to either a full-time staff, or part-time of an individual?				
19.	Are appropriate technical journals subscribed to and made available to both operators and users?				

PERSONNEL SELECTION AND TRAINING

No.	Item	Response			
		Yes	No	N/A	Comments
	<u>Personnel Training</u> **(Continued)**				
20.	Is there a library-type facility to make available: a. computer vendor courses? b. purchased technical courses? c. application-specific material? d. self-instructional training courses? e. video tape material, with an available viewer? f. technical journals and reference material?				

Figure 3-5

USER RELATIONSHIPS

No.	Item	Response			
		Yes	No	N/A	Comments
1.	Does the manager of the small computer system report directly to the management of the principal user area?				
2.	Are the supervisors of the user area involved in the establishment of: a. operating standards and procedures? b. controls and control management? c. priorities and schedules of operation? d. planning for future developments?				
3.	Is there a clear understanding between the operations of the system and the users as to: a. response time? b. turnaround time for reports? c. delivery of output? d. handling of reruns? e. handling of controls? f. system availability?				
4.	Has the adequacy of security of the data files been evaluated with all management concerned?				
5.	Are operational costs identified and measured for all users to consider?				
6.	Are service complaints acted upon to the satisfaction of the users?				
7.	Are problem reports, both for data and operations, distributed and discussed?				
8.	Are the users quickly informed of changes planned to the equipment, systems, procedures, and practices?				
9.	Are user change requests submitted on standard forms or request sheets to clarify the request and to maintain a record of it?				
10.	Is the production support (supplied either by internal Technical Support or vendors) meeting the urgency of the users' requirements?				

QA reviews of large computer systems are complex, and require the interaction of many technical persons and users. QA reviews of small computer systems may possibly be handled by a technical specialist and a knowledgeable user. Both will need to have an understanding of the other's area, however. A QA review is not simply an audit review or a technical analysis. It reviews the combination of control, efficiency, and effectiveness of the system. It tries to answer the questions:

- Is the system operating under adequate control of all aspects?
- Is the system operating efficiently, at the best cost, with the best equipment?
- Is the system operating effectively, giving the user the information that is most useful and helpful?

Figure 3-6, Quality Assurance Functions, is a checklist that includes the principal areas that should be covered in such an analysis.

3.5 THE INTERNAL CONTROL ENVIRONMENT

The internal control environment established by management has a significant impact on the selection of an organization's data processing control procedures and techniques, and their effectiveness. A strong control environment is equally as important for small computer systems as it is for the larger computer systems. Fewer operational, physical, and system controls may be realistic to apply, but may be available in the software, and all aspects must be considered. The data and information in small computer systems is as valuable as that in the larger systems.

This section on "Building a Strong Control Environment" was extracted from the **FTP Technical Library manual "Internal Controls: Volume I, Design, Maintenance, and Assessment."** Much of the information given here is directly applicable to those who are operating small computer systems. Some of the information is on a broader scale, and is presented here as tutorial information for those who manage small computer systems so that the reason for the controls, the nature of the controls, and the surrounding control environment may be apparent. Controls are established over small computer systems, and the applications programs run on them, as an integral part of the larger control environment in the organization.

The control environment is shaped by several factors. Some are clearly visible, like a formal corporate conduct policy statement or an internal audit function. Some are intangible, like the competence and integrity of personnel. Some, such as organizational structure and the way in which management communicates, enforces and reinforces policy, vary so widely among companies that they can be contrasted more easily than they can be compared.

It is difficult to measure the significance of each factor, but it is generally possible to make an overall evaluation. An overall evaluation of a company's internal control environment is a necessary prelude to the evaluation of its control procedures and techniques. It is fundamental to assuring the validity, efficiency, and effectiveness of the data processing operations of any size.

Figure 3-6
(Page 1)

QUALITY ASSURANCE FUNCTIONS

No.	Item	Response			
		Yes	No	N/A	Comments
1.	Is there an assigned Quality Assurance function in the organization?				
2.	Have the QA personnel reviewed the operation and controls of the small computer system and made recommendations?				
3.	Are operations procedures in place to ensure that the programs are run correctly and under control?				
4.	Are standards enforced in the input, operations, and output distribution?				
5.	Are written procedures established and in force to ensure a controlled operation of the system?				
6.	Are adequate security and privacy provisions in place?				
7.	Has a disaster recovery and backup contingency plan been prepared and tested?				
8.	Are the systems and programs considered to be of excellent quality?				
9.	Are internally-developed systems and programs written by persons with adequate experience, and well-documented?				
10.	Are hardware and software contracts monitored to determine that all beneficial clauses are utilized to gain refunds, extra services, etc.?				
11.	Are system development projects tracked and reported to management?				
12.	Are changes, corrections, and modifications to the systems controlled and tested to the same degree as the original systems?				
13.	Is the database well-controlled with adequate automatic recovery procedures?				

QUALITY ASSURANCE FUNCTIONS

No.	Item	Response			
		Yes	No	N/A	Comments
14.	Are procedures established to follow up on all problems within 24 hours of detection?				
15.	Is there a formal method of monitoring new systems and major enhancements to existing systems?				
16.	Are all change requests documented?				
17.	Is there a post-installation audit or review of all systems?				
18.	Is a QA person or a consultant authorized to review all aspects of a system's development, installation, and operation?				
19.	Is a QA review considered to be an essential part of the system operation?				
20.	Do all users and technical personnel participate in QA reviews when requested to do so?				

A weak control environment would make some controls ineffective. For example, individuals in an organization would hesitate to challenge a management override of a specific control procedure. This lessens the possibility of selection of effective control. A strong control environment can have an important bearing on the selection and effectiveness of specific accounting control procedures and techniques.

It is possible for control procedures and techniques to work in a company that has a poor control environment. It is unlikely that management can have reasonable assurance that the broad objectives of internal control are being met, unless the company has an environment that establishes an appropriate level of control consciousness.

The control environment relates to all the employees of a company and even to its suppliers and customers. Leadership in formulating and communicating an appropriate atmosphere of control consciousness must come from the board of directors, its audit committee, and top management. That leadership involves establishing organizational policy, creating an appropriate organizational structure, mandating sound management practices, establishing accountability for performance, and requiring adherence to appropriate standards for ethical behavior, including compliance to applicable laws and regulations. Many companies have found it necessary to formalize such guidance through written policies and procedures. Formalization of such matters is conducive to an environment in which controls are likely to be understood, and to operate effectively.

- **Organizational Structure:**

The organizational structure of a company provides the overall framework for the planning, direction, and control of its operations. In general, it involves reporting relationships, functions to be performed by organizational units, and the authority, responsibilities, and constraints of key positions.

The effectiveness of a company's organizational structure depends on how well it serves as a framework for direction and control of company activities. An effective structure would give appropriate consideration to the following matters:

- Competence of personnel and provision of appropriate resources to discharge the responsibilities assigned, together with a system of measurement of, and accountability for, performance.

- Delegation of responsibility and authority to deal with matters such as goals and objectives, operating functions, organization form, management style, regulatory requirements, and financial reporting standards.

- Budgets and financial reports to facilitate the discharge of assigned responsibilities and monitor the activites at each level in the organizational structure.

- Checks and balances that separate incompatible activities to preclude absolute control by any single individual or unit, provide supervision by higher levels of management, and provide the monitoring of overall company activities.

The larger a company is, and the more complex its operations, the more desirable it is to document the organizational structure. Organization charts, position descriptions, policy statements, and similar documents are frequently used for that purpose.

- **Personnel:**

The internal control environment and the control procedures themselves are highly dependent on the competence and integrity of the company's personnel, the independence of their assigned functions, and their understanding of the prescribed procedures.

These factors are particularly important to the maintenance of an appropriate internal accounting control environment. Dishonest or incompetent employees can render most control procedures inoperative. Misunderstanding of instructions, mistakes of judgment, carelessness, or other personnel factors related to competence and integrity can result in errors in the performance of control procedures. Collusion between employees can circumvent certain control procedures. Similarly, management personnel may often be in a position to circumvent or override control procedures intentionally. Accordingly, management should consider whether the company's policies and procedures with respect to hiring, evaluation, compensation, promotion, training, and so forth, are conducive to the employment of competent, honest personnel.

- **Delegation and Communication of Responsibility and Authority:**

Management should delegate or limit authority in a manner that provides assurance that its responsibilities are effectively discharged. Thus, authority for specific matters should be assigned and limited in a manner that permits an effective review of decisions made. Each level of management might obtain reasonable assurance as to the appropriate exercise of delegated authority through such measures as appropriate reports (audit reports, financial statements, etc.), observation, discussion, consultation, and the organizational structure itself. Each level of management should operate in a similar fashion, delegating authority within reasonable limits while retaining final responsibility. This results in a network of personnel who are specifically authorized to approve or disapprove designated transactions, and who are prohibited from engaging in or approving other specified transactions.

Each level in the organization needs a clear understanding of the authority and responsibilities delegated, and their relationships with respect to others in the organization. There is also a need to know the policies, procedures, and activities that directly and indirectly affect individual responsibilities. Appropriate communications is, therefore, essential to control consciousness. Communications regarding the delegation of responsibility and authority, and related policies and procedures, must be explicit to be effective. Communications need not be written to be explicit, although that may be helpful. The critical test is that those who need to be informed are, in fact, properly informed.

- **Budgets and Financial Reports:**

The formulation and communication of company goals and objectives enables managers to propose courses of action, receive approval and direction, know what is expected of them, and perform in a complementary, unified manner. Budgets and financial reports are tools used in that process. When approved, budgets and longer range plans constitute a form of general authorization. Although the specifics set forth in such budgets and plans will vary with the company's specific circumstances, they should:

- Present for each level of management all material aspects of planned operations for which it has either direct or oversight responsibilities.

- Be segmented in a manner that reflects the assigned responsibilities set forth in the plan or organization.

- Be updated to reflect management's decisions relative to changes in conditions and circumstances.

Financial reports that compare budgeted and actual results, and analyze variances and the managerial action that results from that analysis, may enable management to identify areas where controls may need to be strengthened. They also provide a means for evaluating performance, help provide reasonable assurance that transactions are being executed in accordance with management's authorization, and help develop an attitude of accountability at all levels of the company.

Appropriate reports are a key form of control over the exercise of authority that has been delegated to others. Accordingly, they assume increased significance to management at higher levels in the company whose involvement in day-to-day transactions tends to lessen significantly.

- **Organizational Checks and Balances:**

The concept of checks and balances is inherent in all aspects of the internal control environment -- organizational structure, delegation and communication of responsibility and authority, and budgets and financial reports. The concept has specific application as a general control technique applicable to all accounting cycles.

In evaluating checks and balances in an organization, two particular functions should be carefully considered -- the Financial Control and Internal Audit Functions. Those two functions stand apart from others in the organizational structure in that an important purpose of both is to establish and maintain an appropriate level of control consciousness in the company.

Financial Control Function

The activities of this function might be performed by a combination of organizational segments, for example, controllership, treasury, planning, and information systems. Such activities will also involve different arrays or reporting relationships, depending on the company's organizational structure. The specifics of an effective organizational structure must permit the corporate level executives responsible for the financial control to discharge their reponsibilities to the Chief Executive and the Board.

The financial control function is, by its nature, concerned with the establishment and continuous supervision of the control environment. Activities for which this function should be responsible include the following:

- Design of control procedures and techniques applicable to specific transactions.

- Oversight of specific transactions to assure that they are properly recorded and otherwise satisfy control criteria.

- Design of financial planning and reporting systems that appropriately capture management's plans and the results of actual performance.

- Issuance of reports that appropriately present both planned and actual financial performance.

- Identification and communication of significant variances from management's plan.

Internal Auditing

According to the Institute of Internal Auditors, internal auditing is "an independent appraisal function established within an organization to examine and evaluate its activities as a service to the organization." The standards provide, among other things, that "internal auditors should be independent of the activities they audit." An effective internal auditing function can serve as a high-level organizational control, as well as a constructive and protective link between policy-making levels and operating levels of an organization.

One of the tasks of internal auditing may be the evaluation of internal controls (which include accounting controls) and the determination of whether they are functioning effectively. This includes systems and operational controls in data processing.

- **EDP Considerations:**

The method of data processing used by a company may influence its organizational structure, and the procedures and techniques used to accomplish the broad objectives of internal accounting control. Accordingly, EDP considerations play an important role in evaluating a company's control environment and its control procedures.

The characteristics of computer systems and computerized controls indicate the need for management to understand the exposures and controls for specific business applications and cycles, and to understand the controls in the computer processes themselves. The degree of reliance that can be placed on controls exercised by the computer system is dependent on the degree of control exercised by management over the development and maintenance of the computer system.

Physical concentration of data, concentration of different functions within the EDP activity, and the use of common data by multiple users, are some of the important characteristics of contemporary computer systems. Accordingly, special consideration should be given to three major threats in an EDP environment:

1. The loss of important information through disaster;

2. The ability of a single individual to make unauthorized changes that negate internal accounting controls or permit improper accesses to assets; and

3. The possibility of unintentional loss of assets (for example, loss through pricing errors on sales invoices because of errors in the master price file).

Some of the tasks frequently performed in the EDP process itself are listed below:

- Initiation, authorization, execution, and reporting of transactions according to pre-established rules. Examples might include interest and depreciation calculations, orders to purchase or ship merchandise, and automatic preparation of checks for repetitive payments, such as dividends, employee benefits, or freight settlements.

- Preparation or processing of documents that authorize the use or disposition of assets. This indirect access may occur in connection with transactions that are computer initiated.

- Performance of the full range of accounting functions, that is, recording, classifying, summarizing, and reporting transactions.

- Implementation of accounting controls. Those controls may relate to internally generated transactions, internal processing, or internal files, as well as data submitted for processing.

The wide range of tasks that may be performed by the EDP process emphasizes the importance of proper systems development methods and the participation of management in the development process.

Management should also recognize that computer programs are frequently subject to change. If the change process (or program maintenance) is not controlled, an individual can make unauthorized changes, or can make incorrect changes that can have an unpredictable effect on the data files. For example, internal transactions may be generated; assets may be indirectly accessed by individuals reponsible for accounting for the assets; editing and reporting of errors or exceptions may be subverted. Similarly, to the extent that supervisory programs are changed, and the change process itself is not controlled, unauthorized transactions may be initiated and the reporting of those transactions may be suppressed. Finally, to the extent that direct, unauthorized access to the computer can occur, data programs can be accidentally or intentionally modified or destroyed.

In considering its organizational structure, management should recognize that the development of contemporary systems consists of identifying the company's business requirements from diverse sources and users, and translating them into operational computer instructions. This requires a substantially higher level of coordination among groups within the organization, and among technical disciplines, than was previously required when systems simply supported individual departments.

3.6 ENVIRONMENTAL AND APPLICATION CONTROLS

The objective of internal control is to control events. These events are controlled by a combination of environmental and application controls. Strong environmental controls are essential to the effectiveness of the application controls.

The relationship between environmental and application controls varies from organization to organization. The more centralized the organization, the more that organization relies upon environmental controls. In a highly centralized organization, centralization of most of their functions has the effect of moving control from the application to the environment. For example, a single payroll system for an organization establishes most payroll policies and controls at the environmental level. On the other hand, by decentralizing payroll, many of the payroll functions will be locally designed, and thus become application controls.

The relationship between application and environmental controls is illustrated in **Figure 3-7, Application Controls And Environmental Controls.** This shows that, in a highly centralized organization, a larger portion of controls are environmental while, in a decentralized organization, there are more application-type controls. It also points up the need for much greater attention to be paid to the application controls on small computer systems scattered through the organization.

The strength and enforcement of environmental controls set the control atmosphere in an organization. If senior management establishes a high level of integrity standard for the organization, it will permeate through the application controls. It is the quality and strength of environmental controls, not the quantity, that is important.

3.7 ASSESSING THE ENVIRONMENTAL CONTROL ATMOSPHERE

The control atmosphere in an organization is an intangible element of control. It involves the desire of senior management to establish and implement policy and supporting guidelines relating to the manner in which business is conducted in the organization.

The control atmosphere is influenced by policies and the implementation of guidelines in areas such as:

- Employee Codes of Conduct
- Relationship with Customers
- Relationship with Competitors

Figure 3-7

APPLICATION AND ENVIRONMENTAL CONTROLS

In a Centralized Organization

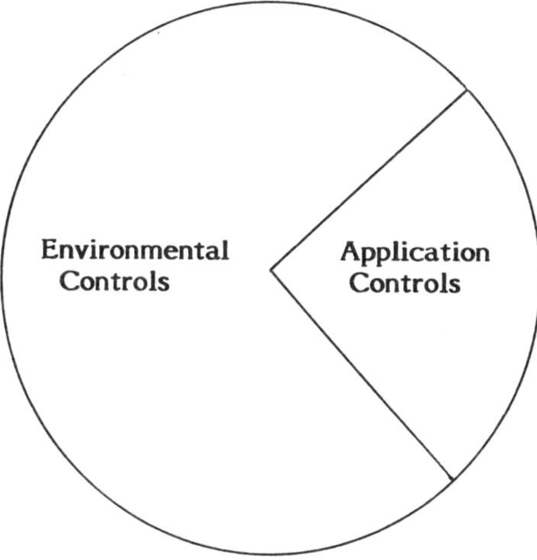

In a Decentralized Organization

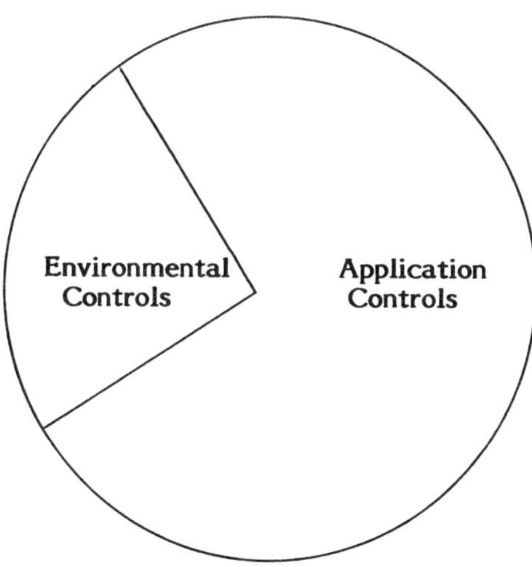

- Meeting the Intent of Federal Regulations
- Reporting of Control Violations to Senior Management
- Enforcement Procedure Over Control Violations

Policies concerning these matters are formalized, documented, and disseminated to all interested parties in many organizations. Some organizations have placed their code of conduct policies in employee handbooks. Some corporations conduct training sessions for all their employees on these codes of conduct and, in instances, make them available to their customers and suppliers.

It is difficult to specifically measure the intent of an organization to have strong internal controls. However, like other "soft" areas, such as morale, it is usually obvious when a strong control atmosphere does or does not exist. **Figure 3-8, Evaluation Of Control Atmosphere,** is a checklist which provides an indication of the strength of the control atmosphere in an organization. In using the checklist, judgment is required because it is difficult to quantitatively define some of the qualitative aspects of management's intent to have a strong control atmosphere.

The results of this checklist should be discussed with senior management. Senior management may wish to use this as a self-assessment checklist to help them assess the control atmosphere in their organization. The following guidelines in assessing the results help provide an indication of the control atmosphere.

The conclusion is based on the number of "Yes" answers to the questions on the checklist. This should only be considered as a guide to the strength of the control environment atmosphere, however, as the numbers themselves are not significant.

GUIDE TO ASSESSING ANSWERS TO FIGURE 3-8

Number of Yes Answers	Strength of Control Atmosphere
19 - 22	Very Strong Control Atmosphere
15 - 18	Strong Control Atmosphere
11 - 14	Average Control Atmosphere
6 - 10	Weak Control Atmosphere
0 - 5	Very Weak Control Atmosphere

Figure 3-8
(Page 1)

EVALUATION OF CONTROL ATMOSPHERE

No.	Item	Response			
		Yes	No	N/A	Comments
1.	Does a formal employee code of conduct policy exist?				
2.	Does a formal policy on internal control exist?				
3.	Has the Board of Directors established an audit committee comprised of outside directors?				
4.	Is the structure of the organization representative of the way things actually happen in the organization?				
5.	Does management receive regular reports on violations of internal control?				
6.	Are violators of the organization's internal control policies and procedures promptly punished?				
7.	Are the expenditures of the organization controlled by a budgetary procedure?				
8.	Are senior members of management required to sign representation letters indicating the adequacy of control in their area of responsibility in the organization?				
9.	Are senior members of management required to sign a statement indicating that they have conformed to the organization's code of conduct policy?				
10.	Is there an internal audit department?				
11.	Does the internal audit department report either directly or indirectly to the audit committee and/or a senior member of management outside the financial area?				
12.	Are audit findings and recommendations, from both internal and external auditors, promptly acted upon?				

Figure 3-8
(Page 2)

EVALUATION OF CONTROL ATMOSPHERE

No.	Item	Response Yes	No	N/A	Comments
13.	Does the organization punish and/or prosecute employees found guilty of fraud and embezzlement of organization assets?				
14.	Does a formal policy exist stating who is responsible for authorizing each type of transaction?				
15.	Are the expense accounts of the senior officers reviewed by other more senior officers or the board of directors?				
16.	Is there a formal procedure for reviewing cost and/or budget overruns?				
17.	Has the organization established formal policies regarding improper use of corporate funds as defined in the Foreign Corrupt Practices Act?				
18.	Does the organization have an open door policy which permits employees to visit any member of management to discuss employee problems and/or grievances?				
19.	Do either auditors or a quality assurance group independently assess the adequacy of controls in computerized business applications?				
20.	Do senior officers of the organization receive, review, and act upon customer complaints?				
21.	Does a procedure exist for reporting losses to members of senior management (Note: The report may be for losses over a stated amount)?				
22.	Are losses consolidated on a regular basis so that management is aware of the magnitude of losses?				

3.8 TYPES OF ENVIRONMENTAL CONTROLS

There are six areas of the **control environment** that can be discussed. The first four are internal accounting control objectives, as included in the Foreign Corrupt Practices Act, and the last two are management control objectives. The six areas of environmental controls are:

Authorization:	Transactions are executed in accordance with management's general or specific authorization.
Recording:	Transactions are recorded as necessary (1) to permit preparation of financial statements in conformity with generally accepted accounting principles or any other criteria applicable to such statements, and (2) to maintain accountability for assets.
Asset Safeguarding:	Access to assets is permitted only in accordance with management's authorization.
Accountability:	The recorded accountability for assets is compared with the existing assets at reasonable intervals and appropriate action is taken with respect to any difference.
Performance:	The organization is operated in an efficient, economical, and effective manner.
Systems Development:	The systems and procedures developed by the organization meet the needs of the organization.

- **Authorization Environmental Controls:**

Authorization to perform an act implies that transactions are executed in accordance with management's general or specific authorization. Authorization by management is at two levels. The first is general authorization, which encompasses the authority to perform an act. The second level is specific authorization, which is the authority to initiate and/or approve a specific transaction.

These levels of authority can be explained by an example. The treasurer of an organization can be delegated the general authority to sign payroll checks. The result of this general authority is that the organization notifies the bank that the treasurer is authorized to sign checks for the payroll account. However, while the treasurer has the authority to sign checks, as a result of management's **general authorization,** that does not permit the treasurer to sign any check that the treasurer so desires. **Specific authorization** is still needed before the treasurer can sign an individual payroll check. This authorization takes effect when an employee is processed through the personnel department and added to the payroll at a specified pay rate. The payroll application produces an employee payroll check which becomes the specific authorization for the treasurer to sign that check.

General authorization is normally an environmental control, and specific authorization is normally an application control. While this is a general rule, there are exceptions.

The types of authority that most firms consider to be **general authorization** by management to execute a transaction are:

- Approval of Annual Operating Plans
- Approval of Annual Operating Budgets
- Approval of Job Descriptions and Organization Charts
- Corporate and Divisional Approved Policies and Procedures Manuals
- Management's Written Policies Outlining Who is Responsible for Specific Assets
- Management's Written Policies Outlining What can be Delegated According to Dollar Limits
- Control Objectives Established for Each Type of Asset
- Approval Levels
- Written Policy Statements on Levels of Authority
- Salary Procedures

The types of authority that most firms consider to be **specific authorization** by management to execute a transaction are:

- Written Mechanism for Delegating Authority (i.e., requirement of an individual delegation for each authorized individual and/or act)
- Signature Authority to Authorize an Event
- Cross-key Control over Sensitive Area (i.e., access to data processing area, bank vault, etc.)
- Restricted Access to Buildings
- Requirement that a Specific Individual Responsible for Assets Establish Control Over the Access to Those Assets (e.g., bonded warehouses, guard forces, alarm systems, fenced-in areas, tool cribs, TV monitors, etc.)

- Standardized Corporate Procedures
- Organizational Charts Illustrating Specific Authority and Access to Assets
- Prenumbered Documents
- Appropriate Segregation of Duties to Preclude Unilateral Control of a Complete Transaction
- Pretransaction Execution Review
- Formal Approval of Capital and Nonroutine Expenditures
- Formal Approval of All Salary Increases
- Requirement for Written Contracts

An organization's general authorization policy should be formalized. This is valuable because:

a. It forces the organization to definitely state its authorization policy;

b. Employees will have in their possession the authorization policy that they are required to utilize and enforce; and

c. It provides positive evidence of compliance to the provisions of the Foreign Corrupt Practices Act.

Figure 3-9, Authorization Environmental Controls, is a checklist that outlines the criteria to be considered in establishing environmental controls over authorization. This checklist can be used for designing and implementing an authorization policy, as well as for assessing the adequacy of those policies.

- **Recording Environmental Controls:**

Formalized recording procedures are needed so that the financial statements adequately reflect the results of transaction processing during a specified period. The objectives of these procedures are to assure the proper recording of all transactions. The proper recording of all transactions is necessary to assure reliable processing results.

The procedures for the proper recording of transactions should define the flow of documents throughout the organization and provide for documenting sufficient information to enable adequate record keeping. These procedures also need to specify the controls over those records.

The record keeping procedures should include all records from the initiation of the source transaction, to the final postings to the general ledger. These are paper documents and bound books in a manual environment, but in a computerized environ-

Figure 3-9
(Page 1)

AUTHORIZATION ENVIRONMENTAL CONTROLS

No.	Item	Response			
		Yes	No	N/A	Comments
1.	Does a policy exist which outlines management's general authorization to access assets?				
2.	Are there specific authorization policies and/or procedures that outline management's specific authorization to access assets?				
3.	Do authorization policies prohibit unauthorized payments or preferential terms and conditions to any foreign government, entity, person, or political action?				
4.	Are annual operating plans prepared and approved by senior management?				
5.	Are annual operating budgets prepared and approved by senior management?				
6.	Are job descriptions established for each position in the organization?				
7.	Do job descriptions establish and limit the amount of authority for each position?				
8.	Are organizational charts prepared and approved by senior management?				
9.	Are salary procedures established and followed?				
10.	Are hiring practices established and followed?				
11.	Is there a controller's manual outlining the financial policies and procedures?				
12.	Is one individual made accountable for each asset?				
13.	Are individuals' authorities limited by a specific dollar limit?				
14.	Are senior officer signatures required on expenditures over a specified dollar limit?				

AUTHORIZATION ENVIRONMENTAL CONTROLS

No.	Item	Response			
		Yes	No	N/A	Comments
15.	Are two or more signatures required for transactions over a certain dollar limit?				
16.	Are employees informed as to the types of commitments they can and cannot make in the name of their organization?				
17.	Are all contracts reviewed by legal counsel?				
18.	Are production/conversion plans and schedules approved?				
19.	Do the By-Laws of the corporation spell out authorization for the purchase and sale of capital assets, securities, and contracts?				
20.	Are the methods of implementing generally accepted accounting principles approved?				
21.	Are financial statements approved by members of senior management before their release?				
22.	Are reports to government agencies approved by members of senior management before their release?				
23.	Are press releases and other documents going to outsiders approved by members of senior management before their release?				

ment, the records may be information entered via a terminal, recorded on machine-readable media, and produced by high-speed printers.

The objectives of recording do not change based on the method of recording (e.g., manual versus automated). However, the methods for recording and the evidence produced by those recordkeeping methods vary significantly. A check includes date, payee, and payor's signature on paper. The evidence of customer number, password, and amount in a cash dispensing terminal is recorded on computer media, such as a magnetic disk or tape.

Figure 3-10, Recording Environmental Controls, outlines the criteria to be considered in establishing environmental controls over recording. This checklist can be used for designing and implementing recording policy, as well as for assessing the adequacy of those policies.

- **Assets Safeguarding Environmental Controls:**

The use of company assets is a necessary part of the day-to-day operations of any organization. The use of those assets should be restricted to authorized personnel. The amount of protection afforded an asset should be related to its liquidity. Cash, being the most liquid of all assets, is highly susceptible to misappropriation while fixed assets, such as buildings, are the least susceptible to misappropriation.

Asset safeguarding refers to security over assets. Security can be both physical and logical security. Physical security is defined as the means that "physically" prevent individuals from gaining access to assets. Logical security includes built-in procedures that individuals must follow, such as the use of passwords on cash-dispensing terminals. These procedures are used to restrict access to assets to authorized individuals. Small computer systems, their programs, and their data files must be considered as valuable assets to an organization.

Physical protection of assets is necessary and may be accomplished through such varied procedures as:

- Storing negotiable documents in secure containers, such as safes, bank vaults, etc.
- Restricting asset access through the use of such physical means as fences, locked areas, buildings, file cabinets, etc.
- Restricting assets access to authorized personnel by providing guards or supervisory review
- Maintaining duplicate copies of critical documents, files, and records in off-site locations
- Dividing assets among multiple areas as opposed to storing it all in a single location
- Storing critical assets, such as precious metals, security, and cash in highly secure fireproof vaults
- Providing Badges identifying authorized employees
- Protecting assets from deterioration from the elements.

Figure 3-10
(Page 1)

RECORDING ENVIRONMENTAL CONTROLS

No.	Item	Response			
		Yes	No	N/A	Comments
1.	Does a complete chart of accounts exist?				
2.	Is each account adequately described to indicate the type of transactions that should be recorded using that account number?				
3.	Are procedures established to determine that transactions are recorded in the appropriate accounting period?				
4.	Do the recorded transactions include the name of the individual accountable for that transaction?				
5.	Are transactions recorded in accordance with generally accepted accounting procedures?				
6.	Is sufficient data recorded with each transaction, so that the processing which occurred in creating the transaction can be reconstructed if necessary?				
7.	Are all negotiable instruments prenumbered?				
8.	Are key documents, such as purchase orders, invoices, etc., prenumbered?				
9.	Is appropriate control maintained over prenumbered documents so that the loss of one or more documents would be recognized and investigated?				
10.	Are controls sufficient to ensure that only actual transactions are recorded?				
11.	Are controls sufficient to ensure that the recorded amounts are correct?				
12.	Are controls sufficient to ensure that all recorded transactions are included in the financial statements?				

RECORDING ENVIRONMENTAL CONTROLS

No.	Item	Response			
		Yes	No	N/A	Comments
13.	Are procedures developed to ensure that the recording of transactions is independent from the authority to initiate or authorize those transactions?				
14.	Are procedures developed to ensure that the record-keeping function is organizationally independent of the function having responsibility for the custody of assets?				
15.	Are procedures developed to ensure that all changes, adjustments, corrections, and alterations to recorded amounts are recorded on a timely basis?				
16.	Are controls sufficient to ensure that these changes, adjustments, corrections, and alterations are correct?				
17.	Are procedures established so that all recorded transactions are properly classified?				
18.	Are procedures established so that all recorded transactions are properly summarized?				
19.	Are procedures established to ensure that transactions are recorded on a timely basis?				
20.	Are procedures established to ensure that recorded transactions will be retained in accordance with the organization's retention procedures?				
21.	Are procedures established to ensure that recorded transactions will be retained in accordance with government regulations?				

Protection of assets may be accomplished through various logical procedures including:

- Hiring procedures that investigate the integrity of personnel in sensitive positions
- Providing insurance to lessen the impact of loss of assets
- Bonding key employees
- Obtaining key-man insurance for essential employees
- Using magnetically encoded cards that must be inserted into equipment to gain access
- Using passwords known only to the authorized individual
- Using a computer-controlled level of processing authority
- Listing the name of a trusted employee on a name and address list so that, if the list is compromised and the people on that list are contacted, the trusted employee will also be contacted. Note that the trusted employee normally uses a special middle initial tied to the file of names being protected.
- Developing disaster plans covering the procedures to be incorporated should a loss of assets occur.

Safeguarding procedures should be documented. These procedures can then be used to substantiate compliance with the Foreign Corrupt Practices Act of 1977. **Figure 3-11, Assets Safeguarding Environmental Controls,** provides the criteria that can be used in designing or investigating asset safeguarding environmental controls.

- **Accountability Environmental Controls:**

Among the four responsibilities outlined in the Foreign Corrupt Practices Act, the accountability responsibility is the one of greatest concern to most organizations. The responsibility for comparing the recorded accountability for assets with the existing assets at reasonable intervals, and taking appropriate action with respect to any difference, belongs to management. Management uses many methods to meet this responsibility. It is normally delegated to supervision, internal auditors, and independent auditors.

Supervisors, members of middle and lower management, are normally accountable for an organization's assets. Responsive and alert first-line supervision is the strongest control for accountability of assets. This is particularly true in the management of small computer systems.

Policies should exist that outline the procedures for supervision to follow in verifying the existence of assets. These procedures will vary based upon the assets and type of business.

Figure 3-11
(Page 1)

ASSETS SAFEGUARDING ENVIRONMENTAL CONTROLS

No.	Item	Response			
		Yes	No	N/A	Comments
1.	Are procedures established to investigate past-due accounts on a timely basis?				
2.	Are procedures established for accounts receivable writeoffs?				
3.	Are procedures established for the sale of scrap materials?				
4.	Are negotiable instruments received restrictively endorsed?				
5.	Are important records protected against physical hazards?				
6.	Is access restricted to offices, plants, etc., according to the value of the assets on those premises?				
7.	Are securities and cash, except those needed for the day-to-day operation of the business, in vaults or equally safe areas?				
8.	Are supplies of unused negotiable instruments stored in a safe place under the custody of a senior member of management?				
9.	Are facsimile signature plates stored in a safe place under the custody of a senior member of management?				
10.	Are unusable or spoiled negotiable instruments voided, and the voided document stored in a secure area until destroyed?				
11.	Is accountability for inventory assigned to a specific individual?				
12.	Is the adequacy of protection over inventory stored at outside locations, such as public warehouses, investigated prior to storing inventory in those locations?				

Figure 3-11
(Page 2)

ASSETS SAFEGUARDING ENVIRONMENTAL CONTROLS

No.	Item	Response			
		Yes	No	N/A	Comments
13.	Do procedures exist for the timely reporting of losses of assets?				
14.	Do procedures exist for the involvement of security audit and/or law enforcement agencies to investigate losses?				
15.	Are losses covered by insurance reported to the insurance companies on a timely basis?				
16.	Are procedures established to physically destroy (e.g., shredding or burning) confidential documents?				
17.	Do procedures exist that require employees to be instructed in the performance of their job tasks?				
18.	Are procedures established to protect the organization's logos and trademarks?				
19.	Are procedures established to protect the organization's copyrights and patents?				
20.	Are job functions adequately documented so that the organization is not dependent upon the continued employment of any single employee?				
21.	Are computerized business applications adequately documented so that the organization is not dependent upon the continued employment of any single employee?				
22.	Have alternate sources of supply been established in the event that one source of supply should become unavailable?				
23.	Are procedures established regarding the entry and movement of visitors through the organization's premises?				

Figure 3-11
(Page 3)

ASSETS SAFEGUARDING ENVIRONMENTAL CONTROLS

No.	Item	Response			
		Yes	No	N/A	Comments
24.	Are procedures established regarding the removal from the organization's premises of any policies, procedures, manuals, correspondence, documentation, or other assets for use by that employee at premises other than those of the organization?				
25.	Are procedures established regarding employees giving talks, writing articles, books, etc., about company products, procedures, and operations?				
26.	Have procedures been established to safeguard employees while on the premises?				
27.	Are procedures established to classify the organization's information according to its importance to individuals?				
28.	Are procedures established to classify the organization's information according to its importance to the organization?				
29.	Has the privacy of information about individuals been adequately protected?				
30.	Have adequate procedures been made to fight disasters, such as fire, flood, etc., should they occur?				
31.	Have alarm devices been installed to protect critical areas against intrusion and/or disasters such as fires?				
32.	Have procedures been established to protect the organization's information from unauthorized access through communication lines?				
33.	Have procedures been established to safeguard the organization's computerized information?				

Accountability is the organization's responsibility to prove that its assets do exist. It also involves determining that the physical assets are in agreement with the organization's records. Accountability requires the periodic comparison of recorded accountability for assets with underlying details. Part of this responsibility is performed by internal or external auditors.

Internal auditing is an independent appraisal function established within an organization to examine and evaluate its activities, as a service to management and the organization. The objective of internal auditing is to assist members of the organization in the effective discharge of their responsibilities. Internal auditing furnishes them with analyses, appraisals, recommendations, counsel, and information concerning the activities reviewed. Internal auditing must take an active part in the review of data processing systems of all types.

Figure 3-12, Accountability Environmental Controls, outlines the criteria to be considered in establishing environmental controls over accountability of assets. This checklist can be used for designing and implementing accountability policy, as well as for assessing the adequacy of those policies.

- **Performance Environmental Controls:**

The Foreign Corrupt Practices Act does not include controls over performance. However, the operational performance of an organization is of direct concern to management. Performance controls help assure the effective, efficient, and economical operation of the organization. Their establishment is of critical importance to the successful operation of small computer systems.

The controls that govern performance are called by many names including:

- Standards
- Guidelines
- Procedures
- Operating Manuals
- Work Programs
- Performance Reviews
- System Analysis
- Personnel Reviews

Most performance controls originate as a result of either good or bad work practice. If certain practices are found to be the best way to perform work, they are then translated into performance controls (e.g., standards, guidelines, etc.) in order to assure that good practices are continued. If poor practices have resulted in inefficient, ineffective, or uneconomical means of doing work, performance controls are established to avoid the recurrence of those poor practices.

The penalty for inadequate performance standards is the unnecessary expenditure of resources. The counter-argument to performance controls is that they inhibit initiative and creativity. Therefore, management must make decisions on the benefits of performance controls versus any inhibiting factors they may have on restricting people's ability to use good judgment.

ACCOUNTABILITY ENVIRONMENTAL CONTROLS

No.	Item	Response			
		Yes	No	N/A	Comments
1.	Is there an independent audit function established to independently compare the recorded accountability for assets with the existing assets?				
2.	Does internal audit make the comparison of recorded accountability for assets with the existing assets at reasonable intervals?				
3.	Are the internal audit reports made available to senior management?				
4.	Are the internal audit reports sent to the manager of the affected areas?				
5.	Do the organization's independent auditors have access to the internal audit reports?				
6.	Are individual assets identified, and is that identification recorded?				
7.	Is the physical location of all assets recorded?				
8.	When the comparison is made between the recorded accountability for assets and the existing assets, is that task properly documented?				
9.	Do procedures establish a specified time period in which appropriate action must be taken with respect to any differences between recorded accountability for assets and the existence of those assets?				
10.	Is the appropriate action taken with respect to any differences recorded, together with the reasons for those actions?				
11.	Are the consequences under the Foreign Corrupt Practices Act arising from differences between recorded accountability for assets with the existing assets evaluated, and appropriate action taken?				

Figure 3-12
(Page 2)

ACCOUNTABILITY ENVIRONMENTAL CONTROLS

No.	Item	Response			
		Yes	No	N/A	Comments
12.	Do procedures specify the methods for this comparison, such as counts of physical inventory observed by auditors, confirmation of accounts receivable, etc.?				
13.	Is a single individual made accountable for each asset?				
14.	Are procedures established so that the individual will verify the existence of assets at regular intervals?				

Figure 3-13, Performance Environmental Controls, outlines the criteria to be considered in establishing environmental controls over performance. This checklist can be used for designing and implementing performance policies and procedures, as well as for assessing the adequacy of those policies and procedures.

- **Program Development Environmental Controls:**

The programs and systems of an organization are established to meet the needs of individual users. For example, computer systems should provide users with needed information on a timely basis, and facility design should meet production and office needs.

Frequently, good programs and systems are established but erode over a period of time. This erosion is due to the inability of the program/system to change with business requirements. The importance of a good program/system cannot be underestimated in achieving success for an organization.

Program/systems are established to meet specific objectives using an authorized set of activities. These activities include departments, people, equipment, funds, space, etc. Program/system controls are designed to ensure that those objectives are met. It is through controls of this type that management is assured it receives value and profitability from their programs and systems.

Figure 3-14, Program/Systems Environmental Controls, outlines the criteria to be considered in establishing environmental controls over program development. This checklist can be used by individuals responsible for designing and implementing program policies and procedures, as well as individuals responsible for assessing the adequacy of those policies and procedures.

Figure 3-13
(Page 1)

PERFORMANCE ENVIRONMENTAL CONTROLS

No.	Item	Response			
		Yes	No	N/A	Comments
1.	Does the organization have a policy to hire competent people possessing the needed skills to perform the job for which they are hired?				
2.	Does the organization provide employees with sufficient training to keep their skills current?				
3.	Is each employee's authority and responsibility clearly stated and communicated to them?				
4.	Is each employee's performance regularly assessed and reviewed with the employee?				
5.	Is there a suggestion system established so that employee suggestions on improving performance can be gathered?				
6.	Are suggestions promptly reviewed and implemented where appropriate?				
7.	Does the organization have a policy requiring a cost/benefit study before embarking upon a new program?				
8.	Does management monitor new programs to determine if those new programs achieve the cost/benefit expectations?				
9.	Is there a policy on evaluating controls from a cost/benefit viewpoint?				
10.	Are there policies requiring implementation schedules for production?				
11.	Are schedules established for the implementation of new projects?				
12.	Are schedules regularly monitored, and variances from schedules investigated with appropriate action taken?				
13.	Are budgets established for all projects and departments?				

Figure 3-13
(Page 2)

PERFORMANCE ENVIRONMENTAL CONTROLS

No.	Item	Response			
		Yes	No	N/A	Comments
14.	Are variances from the budget reviewed by management and action taken where appropriate?				
15.	Are there procedures for cross-training personnel so that two or more people are qualified for each job?				
16.	Are employees required to account for their time and activities as a basis for measuring performance?				
17.	Are job functions adequately documented so that new personnel can take over existing job functions?				
18.	Are systems adequately documented so that they are not dependent upon specific individuals?				
19.	Do procedures require that adequate maintenance be reviewed on equipment?				
20.	Do procedures require that adequate maintenance be required on fixed assets?				
21.	Do procedures require that adequate maintenance be provided for systems?				

Figure 3-14
(Page 1)

PROGRAM/SYSTEMS ENVIRONMENTAL CONTROLS

No.	Item	Response			
		Yes	No	N/A	Comments
1.	Are measurable objectives established for each new program or system?				
2.	Is a post-implementation audit made for all new programs and systems to determine whether or not those objectives were met?				
3.	Are computer systems developed using a system development life cycle process?				
4.	Are projects scheduled using a critical path technique to be assured the implementation schedule is realistic?				
5.	Is the user required to "sign-off" on new programs and systems prior to implementation?				
6.	Is the user required to "sign-off" on the program/system costs prior to implementation?				
7.	Is the user required to "sign-off" on the program/system method of implementation prior to implementation?				
8.	Are user personnel actively involved in those systems/programs that they do not develop themselves?				
9.	Is the user an active participant in contract negotiations for contracted services?				
10.	Does the user "sign-off" prior to accepting new program/systems in their area?				
11.	Do procedures require competitive bidding for systems/programs that are not developed by employees?				
12.	Are procedures established that can stop program/systems during the implementation phases if they do not meet the stated objectives?				

PROGRAM/SYSTEMS ENVIRONMENTAL CONTROLS

No.	Item	Response			
		Yes	No	N/A	Comments
13.	Do procedures require that all changes to contracts be specified in writing?				
14.	Are measures of performance established for new program/systems?				
15.	Are those measures of performance continually monitored during the operation of the new program/system?				
16.	Are customer complaints about a system/program acted upon by senior management?				
17.	Do procedures require the collection and recording of performance information on a regular basis as part of the evaluation system?				
18.	Are programs established to identify and measure adverse side effects associated with a program/system inefficiency?				
19.	Is an annual operating plan prepared?				
20.	Is an annual budget prepared?				
21.	Is a long-range plan prepared (e.g., three to five years)?				
22.	Is a long-range budget prepared (e.g., three to five years)?				

SECTION 4

AUDITING CONSIDERATIONS

SECTION OVERVIEW

The rapid growth of small computer systems has added a new challenge to the auditor's task. Most control and audit procedures have been designed for large-scale computers. The auditor attempting to review a small computer system, using the large computer review methods, will find many of the controls not applicable or uneconomical, and many of the audit practices ineffective. The small computer poses some audit risks not present in a large computer site. The auditor needs to develop an audit approach that addresses the risks and controls of a small computer environment and then develop audit tools and techniques designed for that environment.

This section discusses the central issues of a small computer environment. Suggestions are given on how to approach the audit of a small computer system. The differences between small computer systems and larger computers are discussed from the audit viewpoint. A systematic, four-phased approach of involvement in small computer audits is given. Some of these methods are not available for the smallest systems but are available for the more powerful small computers. Auditing distributed processing systems is also discussed. The following worksheets and checklists are provided:

Figure 4-2: **Existing Data Worksheet**

Figure 4-6: **Self-Evaluation on Distributed System's Maturity**

Figure 4-7: **Distributed Hardware Concerns**

Figure 4-8: **Distributed Processing Concerns**

Figure 4-9: **Distributed Data Concerns**

Figure 4-10: **Distributed Control Concerns**

Figure 4-11: **Distrubuted Security Concerns**

Figure 4-13: **Systems Development Control**

Figure 4-14: **Systems Documentation Control**

Figure 4-15: **Hardware Reliability Control**

Figure 4-16: **Software Reliability Control**

4.1 HOW TO APPROACH THE AUDIT

The audit of small computer systems is similar in principle to the audit of larger computers, but many of the practical audit methods are different because of the limitations of the smaller systems. Small computers pose some audit problems that may not exist in the larger installations. These problems are more relative than absolute, since the larger of the small computer systems are as readily audited as the average large computer. Auditors usually need to be able to change their audit approach when reviewing a small computer environment. Some of the auditing problems with small computer systems are:

- **Risks Unknown:** Control checklists, audit programs, and risk lists have done much to help the auditor identify the risks in a large computer environment. These are not the same risks or the same severity of risks that exist in a small computer environment. It is possible that both management and audit personnel are not aware of the types or severity of risks faced in a small computer installation. Therefore, the control and audit effort in those installations may not address the more serious risks.

- **Audit Software Packages Less Available:** Audit software packages are written for the large computer installation and primarily large IBM computers. Fewer audit software packages are available for the small computer systems.

- **Multiple Vendors:** The auditor, both internal and external, may be faced with a variety of small computer systems. It is more difficult for the auditor to justify investing the time and effort needed to understand the characteristics of a small computer system when the auditor's organization or client may have small computers from many vendors.

- **Lack of Internal Control Review Aids:** Fewer checklists, guidelines, and audit programs are written for the small computer. Therefore, the auditor may not have guidelines to follow in evaluating internal control.

- **Less Reliable Hardware and Software:** The lack of control circuitry and hardware, and control procedures in testing software, make the operating environment less reliable for a small computer than for the larger computers. In large computer installations, the auditors have been able to devote most of their effort to application auditing. Because of the uncertain reliability of hardware and software in the small computer environment, the auditor may have to devote a much larger portion of the audit resources to verifying the hardware and software controls.

- **Unskilled Users:** Auditors in large computer installations may rely upon the skills of the data processing personnel to prevent and detect problems. In many installations, these people have done an exceptionally good job in spite of the lack of control standards. Unskilled users in small computer installations may not be aware of the need to control many of the risk situations which have common controls in large installations.

- **Minimal Audit Literature:** There is little literature in professional auditing publications on the concerns of, and solutions to, small computer audits. Therefore, many auditors are not aware of some of the significant differences between the audits of large computers and small computers.

- **Minimal Audit Tools and Techniques:** Few auditors audit small computer installations. Most of the auditing that is performed is done around the computer rather than through reviewing the controls within the computer system. For this reason, audit methods and practices for auditing small computers have not been sufficiently developed, leaving the effort to develop the approach to those few audit groups actively involved in auditing small computer systems.

- **Lack of Small Computer System Audit Skills:** For all of the above reasons, most auditors lack the skills needed to audit effectively in a small computer environment.

The solution to these problems is to follow the audit approach recommended in this section which is designed to address the control issues in the environment.

For the smaller, standalone computer systems, these differences are marked. Some operations have only one or two persons using the computer, and there is little concern or time for control. For systems handling considerable financial data, however, and for systems connected in a distributed network in a large organization, there may be strong internal controls and considerable management interest in control. In such installations, with sophisticated small computer systems, there is little difference between their operation and the operation of the larger computer systems. Standard data processing controls can be enforced and audit methods can be used, such as are described in detail in the **FTP Technical Library manuals:**

Internal Controls - Volume I, Design, Maintenance, and Assessment

- Volume II, Control Descriptions

Auditing Computer Systems (Three Volumes)

Much of the material in this section is taken from those manuals.

- **Approaching the Audit of Small Computer Systems:**

Organizations that have done little or no EDP auditing of their small computer systems need a logical sequence of steps for involvement into the control and audit of their data processing systems. These steps for involvement are the same for small computer systems and for large computer systems. The difference is only in the limitations of the small computer operating systems and application programs. Adaptation of the approaches is usually necessary.

The problem of approaching systematic audit procedures is multifaceted, because it includes:

a. selection of areas of involvement;

b. selection of personnel to perform the task;

c. training of existing auditing and data processing personnel;

d. support and education of management as to the object and scope of EDP auditing; and

e. the restructuring of the audit tools and techniques used to fit the smaller systems.

Organizations that have become successful in EDP auditing tend to follow a four-phased approach of involvement. These phases are:

1. **Use of Existing Reports,** extracts and other data currently available from the data processing department.

2. **Use of Computer Audit Software,** to provide independence in obtaining the same types of data outlined in one above.

3. **Use of Advanced Audit Techniques,** whereby the auditor can use the computer to audit the applications.

4. **Concurrent Auditing,** where continual monitoring routines analyze transactions and select questionable items for audit follow-up.

These phases are outlined in **Figure 4-1, Four Phases of EDP Auditing,** with an approximate timeframe for advancing through the various phases. All organizations should progress to the second phase as rapidly as possible, but advancement from that point depends on risk and scope of the organization's data processing systems, together with a commitment on the part of management to assign the necessary resources to advance to the more sophisticated aspects of EDP auditing.

PHASE ONE: Use of Existing Data

The needs of internal auditors tend to parallel the needs of organizational management and data processing applications system users. The types of questions that concern management regarding control of systems also concern the auditor. Both management and auditors require the same data to substantiate the authenticity of the data processing.

There are six categories of data processing reports that the auditor should consider for an audit. These reports are frequently produced regularly by the computer

Figure 4-1

FOUR PHASES OF EDP AUDITING

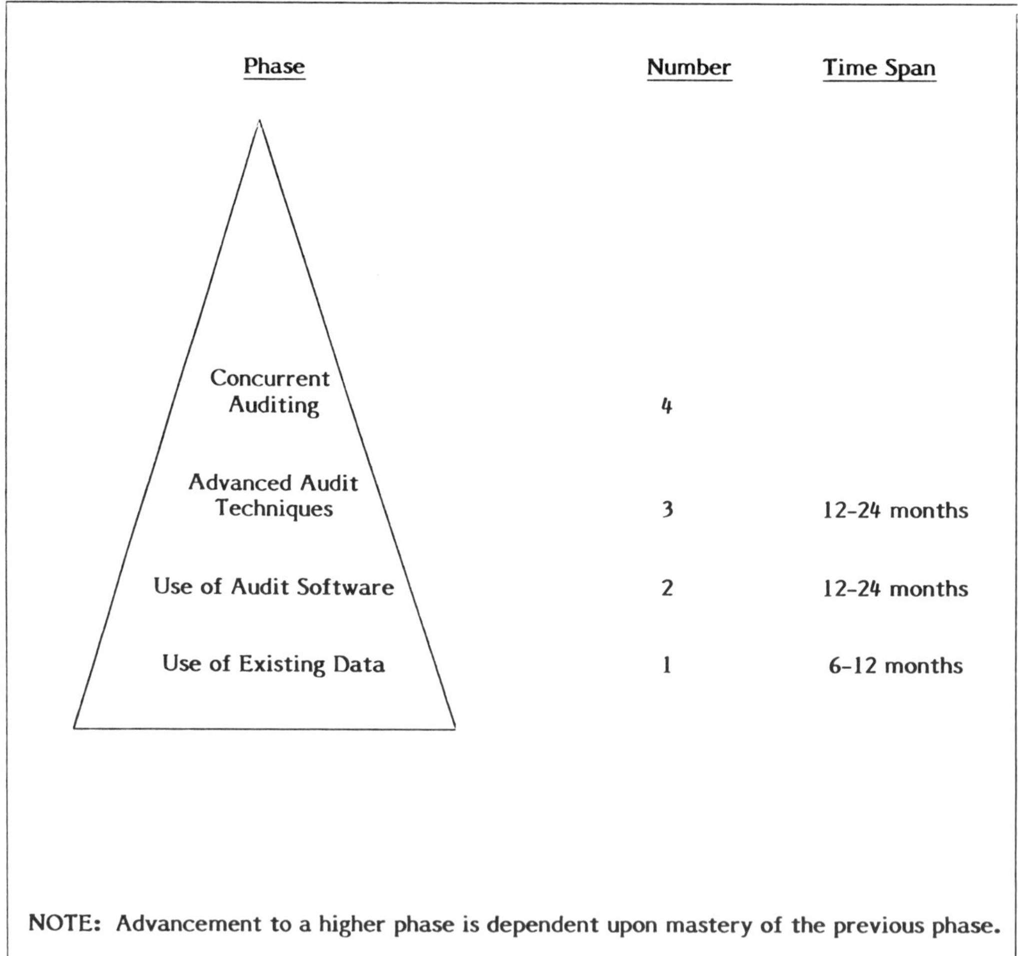

operations for review by management. It is feasible for the auditor to use these same reports to obtain better analyses of data with less auditing effort. The six categories of reports are:

1. **Regular System Reports:** Those reports that are produced on a regular basis (e.g., daily, weekly, monthly, etc.).

2. **Special System Extracts:** Those extracts that have been written for a unique purpose, by a requesting group, to meet a special need. Some of these may be run on demand, while others are prepared for a one-time basis. Most systems groups will retain these programs for future need should a similar request occur.

3. **System Exception Reports:** Reports that are regularly prepared by computer systems for irregular items. Examples are: (a) error scrolls indicating problems with input records or intermediate system records; (b) special restart-type reports where the system is unable to handle a specific record and must delete that record from the system; and (c) reports associated with some special entry point to enter records under unusual circumstances.

4. **System Data Reported by Other Applications:** Frequently data prepared by one system is fed into another system for additonal analysis and reporting. For example, billing systems data is often used for special sales reporting systems to analyze movement of certain products.

5. **System Data Reported by Software Systems:** Within the hierarchy of software supplied by vendors are a variety of analysis programs. Among these are systems that provide considerable data about the use of programs, and data which might be of interest to auditors for special analyses.

6. **Extracts Done by Public Accountants:** Most public accounting firms audit software systems which they use in conducting their audits. Many times a CPA firm is willing to share these extract programs with internal auditors.

Figure 4-2, Phase One: Existing Data Worksheet, can be completed by internal auditors for each system under audit. The form calls for the listing of reports of each type, together with a brief statement of their purpose, frequency of issuance of report (daily, weekly or monthy), the date that report is issued (for example, first Tuesday, 15th, etc.), and the individual to which the report is delivered. An internal auditor in charge of an audit involving data supplied by that computer system can then, at a glance, determine whether or not any of those reports would be of value in meeting the audit objectives set for that particular audit.

Figure 4-2

PHASE ONE: EXISTING DATA

Type of Existing Data	Purpose of Report	Frequency	Date Issued	Delivered To:
Regular System Reports				
1.				
2.				
3.				
4.				
Special System Extracts				
1.				
2.				
3.				
4.				
System Exception Reports				
1.				
2.				
3.				
4.				
System Data Reported By Other Application Systems				
1.				
2.				
System Data Reported By Software Systems				
1.				
2.				
Extracts Done By Public Accounts				
1.				
2.				

PHASE TWO: Use of Audit Software

"Audit software" is a term given to special languages or programs devised for use by auditors. The objective of these languages is to permit auditors to extract data from application files for audit purposes. The reason for using special languages are twofold:

1. The languages use terminology familiar to auditors,

2. They contain some special capabilities not present in current extract languages.

These special audit languages are provided by major public accounting firms and several software houses. Most large software houses have addressed themselves to auditing problems. Some of the major public accounting firms provide these special audit languages to their clients at no cost, and some at a very nominal cost. The software houses lease them at prices designed to provide them with a profit, but the prices may be attractive because the costs are distributed over a number of customers.

Currently, there are approximately twenty different audit software languages available. A number of them can be used on small computer systems. In addition to the ease of use and the provision of some special capabilities, the prime purpose of an audit software language is to provide the auditor with an independent method of obtaining data for audit purposes by a known sampling procedure. In Phase One, we saw that auditors could satisfy most of their needs from existing reports. The disadvantage, for audit purposes, of using existing reports is that they may have been modified without the knowledge of the auditor. Thus, the main items that the auditor is looking for might be deleted or changed on the report that the auditor sees. On the other hand, if the auditor can obtain the information independently of the data processing personnel, there is considerably more assurance that the auditor is examining the entire population of data.

Prior to obtaining the necessary knowledge and background to write one's own extracts, it is necessary to obtain an understanding of both data processing principles and the applications under audit. For these reasons, it is strongly advised that the auditor spend a six to twelve month period working with existing data processing reports prior to selecting and using their own audit software package. Through the use of existing reports and the study of existing applications, the auditor gains an appreciation for the type of data available, as well as the files in which that data is located. Audit software is file dependent, so that, until an auditor has a good appreciation of the files within an application, the use of audit software is not practical.

Figure 4-3, Phase Two: Steps in the Use of Audit Software, outlines the steps involved for an internal audit department to obtain an audit software package. The steps are abbreviated, but they provide guidance as to the method of selecting and using an audit software package. Many of the existing packages are not designed for use on small computer systems.

Modern business systems rely on computer applications, so it is necessary for auditors to have an independent means of extracting data for audit purposes. This extraction is best accomplished by selecting and implementing an audit software package under the auditor's control.

PHASE TWO: STEPS IN THE USE OF AUDIT SOFTWARE

1. Obtain the following data about your organization's EDP capability:

   a. Computer Configuration

   b. Data File and Database Techniques

   c. Vendor's Software Systems Installed

   d. Availability of EDP Facilities to Auditors.

2. Review audit software systems available for small computer systems.

3. Obtain the following data about these audit software systems:

   a. Computer Configuration Required to Operate

   b. Data File and Database Methods that the System Can Access

   c. Operating Systems Features Required.

4. Match the characteristics of items one and three.

5. Select a suitable audit software system.

6. Train auditors and EDP support personnel in the system.

7. Specify, write, test, and execute programs to support the organization's audit objectives.

PHASE THREE: Use Of Advanced Audit Techniques

The four phases of EDP auditing outlined in Figure 10-1 present an approach for involvement by auditors in data processing. The movement to each more advanced step is dependent upon mastery of the previous step.

The first two phases of computer auditing (use of existing data and audit software) are dependent upon the data elements contained in the computer files of applications. These techniques follow the historic trend of auditing by looking at events that have occurred and analyzing the accuracy of those transactions and their conformity to organization policy and procedures.

The term "advanced audit techniques" is used in this manual in the context of tests of operation. The objective of these techniques is to verify the processing rules. The findings are more compliant in nature than substantive in relation to the financial statements of the organization. These techniques are using the computer itself to audit the computer operations.

The use of these advanced techniques requires a detailed knowledge of the computer application and of data processing practices. Prior to implementing these techniques, the auditor needs to proceed through the same steps as those a computer systems designer performs in developing a new computer application. Certain techniques introduce audit test data into the processing of live production data. For example, it is difficult to evaluate on-line real-time systems effectively without seeing the results of data processed in that environment. It does offer an element of risk, however, for without careful planning, live data and summary totals could be inadvertently modified. Most of the advanced audit techniques have been pioneered by data processing personnel who have moved into internal audit functions. The techniques are variations of proven data processing testing and control techniques.

The following characteristics in an organization appear to be those that make it feasible to utilize some of these advanced techniques:

a. Proven experience in the Phase One and Phase Two Steps in computer auditing by the internal audit department.

b. One or more data processing professionals under the control of the general auditor.

c. A data processing department that recognizes the need for computer audit and control.

d. A top management that recognizes the need for accurate, detailed audit and control.

e. Computer systems involving large amounts of organization funds, with an associated large exposure for loss (e.g., large computerized billing accounts receivable system).

Figure 4-4, Phase Three: Examples of Advanced Audit Techniques, lists some examples of advanced audit techniques. The chart lists the name of each technique and a brief description of the purpose for using that technique. These advanced techniques are described in more detail in the Auditing Computer Systems manual.

PHASE THREE: EXAMPLES OF ADVANCED AUDIT TECHNIQUES

Technique	Purpose
1. Integrated Test Facility (ITF)	To comply with the organization's policies and procedures.
2. Extended Records	To provide a complete audit trail by adding the necessary data to records.
3. Transaction Tagging	To determine the path through a computer system of a preselected transaction.
4. Simulation	To show a comparison with a real processing case.
5. Recompiles and Compares	To provide assurance that the correct programs are in operation.
6. Mapping	To examine for hidden source code inserted for purposes of unauthorized transactions.

PHASE FOUR: Concurrent Auditing

The advent of computerized systems has had two impacts on the traditional periodic audit philosophy. First, the lack of clerical people to continually review the functions of processing has meant that it is easier for major errors to go undetected for some time. Therefore, if the auditor is to make a significant and practical test of the system, he must review on a more continuous basis, rather than merely selecting one week or one accounting period per year. Second, by properly using the computer to perform some of the audit steps, the magnitude of the task of the individual auditor can be reduced to the point where it is feasible to do more continuous auditing.

The concurrent auditing concept provides for computer programs to do continual analysis of data. The results of these analyses will provide auditors with transactions for further analysis. The criteria for selecting these transactions for audit purposes is determined by the auditors themselves. Management may desire that line operating personnel also use the output data from these analysis routines on a regular basis. If this is followed, the auditor becomes a secondary user of the concurrent techniques.

Figure 4-5, Phase Four: Examples of Concurrent Audit Techniques, lists three of the more popular techniques. These are also discussed in more detail in the Auditing Computer Systems Manual. These techniques are only available in a practical way on the largest of the small computer systems or on distributed systems with direct communications to a large central computer.

4.2 AUDITING DISTRIBUTED PROCESSING SYSTEMS

The concept of distributed data processing systems implies a decentralized approach to data processing. The distributed concept places computer power where it is most effective in meeting the needs of the user. User responsiveness is a key part of distributed data processing.

The audit of a distributed data system has many similarities to the audit of a computer center. In conducting the audit, the auditor should equate the distributed system with a distributed data center, as the distributed system is, in effect, a distributed computer center. The audit of a distributed system is the audit of the general controls over the processing of the distributed system. However, as with other advanced data processing technology, there is a migration of control from application to environmental.

The environmental controls in an advanced data processing environment assume much greater importance than in a batched environment. The review of a distributed data system is primarily a review of environmental controls. The assessment of the environmental controls will affect the review of the controls over the applications operating in a distributed data environment.

This section discusses distributed systems from an auditor's perspective. It is important for the auditor to be aware of exactly what is being distributed and to review the "distributed data processing system" in order to learn precisely what is distributed. After this determination, the audit and control problems can be put into their proper perspective.

PHASE FOUR: EXAMPLES OF CONCURRENT AUDIT TECHNIQUES

Technique	Purpose
1. System Control Audit Review File (SCARF)	To collect data on a regular basis by predetermined criteria for comparison and further investigation. Also, to plot trends.
2. Audit Module	To review all transactions for the purpose of selecting transactions for audit follow-up based on predetermined criteria.
3. Imbedded Systems Extraction Facilities	To provide accounting and analysis data on use of programs and files.

Thus, we need to examine the characteristics of a distributed system in order to understand the audit and control problems of that system. The characteristics of a distributed system can be divided into five areas:

1. Assignable Resources

2. Autonomy in Communications

3. Transparent Technology

4. Autonomy in Local Processing

5. Integrated Operating Systems

It would be difficult in today's data processing environment to find many, if any, examples of a distributed system with all five characteristics present. Most distributed systems today incorporate one or two of the distributed characteristics.

- **Audit and Control Concerns of Distributed Processing Systems**

The **control concerns** presented by a distributed data processing system include:

- The ability of technology to be responsive to the distributed system requirements;
- The ability to coordinate data updates used by several units when the data files are distributed;
- The ability to control updates when many users will be vying for the same data resources at the same time;
- Maintaining the service level required by users;
- Developing accepted priority systems for allocation of resources;
- Maintaining the integrity of software systems in a distributed environment.

The **auditing concerns** in a distributed data processing system environment include:

- Obtaining auditors with sufficient skills to effectively audit in this environment;
- Devloping audit tools and techniques that are effective in this environment;

- Having auditors with sufficient experience to be able to evaluate the effectiveness of controls in this environment;

- Recognizing potential control problems in a new technology.

There are no easy answers to these control and audit concerns. The one step that is indisputable is that, unless auditors get involved early, their opportunities to contribute to the success of distributed systems will be nonexistent. With each new step in technology, the integrity of the system becomes more dependent upon the adequacy of the automated system of controls.

- **Audit Approach**

What is needed in the audit approach of a distributed system is an assessment of the system being installed versus the "ideal" distributed system. We can do this by looking at the aspects of the system that are distributed.

An auditor audits applications, not the characteristics of a technology. Viewing a distributed system from an auditor's perspective, there are five parts of an application operation that can be distributed. These are:

1. Hardware

2. Processing

3. Data

4. Control

5. Security

The audit approach for a distributed system is dependent upon which of the areas is distributed. Each area will be discussed individually.

a. **Distribution of Hardware:** It would be impractical to have a distributed data processing system if hardware was not distributed. Therefore, the first prerequisite of a distributed system is the distribution of hardware. This poses the potential audit and control problem of having assets and resources distributed at many remote sites.

b. **Distribution of Processing:** Again, it would be difficult to conceive of a distributed data processing system without distributing processing capabilities. The amount and location of processing capabilities can vary, but processing must be distributed from the central location. The amount of processing distributed determines the degree of control and audit concern.

c. **Distribution of Data:** One major audit and control concern is the distribution of data. It is possible to divide logical databases into multiple physical databases. This poses problems of coordination and reconciliation between the distributed physical databases. The problem is magnified when the same data is retained in multiple locations. The problem is one of keeping redundant data current.

d. **Distribution of Control:** When hardware, processing, and data are distributed, control is likewise distributed. This provides advantages and disadvantages. The major advantage is the segregation of control among many units. However, this same advantage has the disadvantage that, as the unit gets smaller in size, the ability of people to manipulate systems increases. This is because, in small units, responsibility is centered around a few key people.

e. **Distribution of Security:** Centralization of data processing has enabled large amounts of resources to be expended on making the central data center secure. Measures that are uneconomical in small locations become economical in central locations. This, coupled with the fact that distributed systems normally involve heavy data movement, results in a challenge to maintain the security of the system.

The first step in an audit of a distributed system is then to assess what areas of the system are distributed. The five areas of a distributed system (as seen from an audit perspective) become the tools for measuring the areas and amount of distribution.

Before beginning the audit, the auditor must first examine the total distributed system and measure the distribution of each area. Once measured, the results of that estimation should be placed on **Figure 4-6, Self-Evaluation on Distributed System's Maturity**. This worksheet provides guidance in using the audit program for each of the five audit areas. If a particular area is not distributed, it can be audited in the conventional manner. The more an area is distributed, the more need there is to look at it from a new perspective. The new perspective is to examine the distributed area independent of the applications run on the system.

The auditor should review each of the five areas, rate them according to these five categories, and then plot the ratings on the worksheet. The five categories are:

1. **Highly Distributed:** Meets the "ideal" distributed system characteristics.

2. **Distributed:** Comes close to the "ideal" characteristics of a distributed system.

3. **Mixed:** Has some of the characteristics of a distributed system and some of the characteristics of a centralized system.

4. **Centralized:** System is basically a centralized system with a few distributed characteristics.

5. **Highly Centralized:** Has practically no characteristics of a distributed system.

Figure 4-6

SELF-EVALUATION ON DISTRIBUTED SYSTEM'S MATURITY

	Hardware	Processing	Data	Control	Security
Highly Distributed					
Distributed					
Mixed					
Centralized					
Highly Centralized					

The ratings can be considered as follows:

1. <u>Hardware</u>

- **Highly Distributed:** If there is no central computer controlling the system, it is a highly distributed hardware network.
- **Distributed:** If the hardware is primarily autonomous, but reverts to a slave/master relationship at times, the rating should be distributed.
- **Mixed:** If the rater is unsure between a distributed and centralized rating, a mixed rating would be appropriate.
- **Centralized:** If terminals have the capability to perform some autonomous processing, but it is basically a slave/master relationship, the assessment should be centralized.
- **Highly Centralized:** If the central computer has a slave/master relationship with terminals, the system is highly centralized.

2. <u>Processing</u>

- **Highly Distributed:** A completely autonomous processing by decentralized units gets a highly distributed rating.
- **Distributed:** Most of the distributed processing is autonomous with some centralized direction.
- **Mixed:** Part of the time processing is centralized and part of the time distributed.
- **Centralized:** Mostly centralized direction with the terminal performing a few autonomous operations.
- **Highly Centralized:** A centralized directed processing, where the terminals perform tasks assigned by the central unit, gets a highly centralized rating.

3. <u>Data</u>

- **Highly Distributed:** The physical data is under the complete jurisdiction of the remote area.
- **Distributed:** The data is physically located at the remote area, but the central system retains a degree of control over the accuracy and completeness of data.

- **Mixed:** The data is at the remote site, but under the complete control of the central unit.

- **Centralized:** The data is located at the central site, but accessible by the remote area.

- **Highly Centralized:** The data is located at the central site and not accessible by the remote area.

4. Control

- **Highly Distributed:** The complete control of the local system resides with the local manager.

- **Distributed:** Control is under the direction of the local manager, but it follows central guidelines.

- **Mixed:** Control is performed locally but ultimately remains at the central location.

- **Centralized:** Control is at the central location but operation is done remotely.

- **Highly Centralized:** Both control and operation is run from the central location.

5. Security

- **Highly Distributed:** Security is under the control of the local manager.

- **Distributed:** Control is under the direction of the local manager but following central guidelines.

- **Mixed:** Security is under the direction of the local manager but controlled by the central group.

- **Centralized:** Security is under the operation of the central group but remains a close relationship with the local manager.

- **Highly Centralized:** Security is under the complete control of the centralized group.

From this criteria, the auditor can rate the five years according to one of the five ratings. This rating will serve three purposes:

1. An evaluation of the amount of actual distribution occurring in the computer environment.

2. A prioritization of which distributed system's characteristics should be audited first; the most highly distributed one being the one audited first.

3. Guidance as to whether the audit should occur remotely or centrally.

The following will discuss how to audit each of these five areas.

- **Distributed Hardware Auditing Concerns**

The audit and control concerns of hardware in a distributed system are similar to those in a conventional computer center. The specific concerns center around accountability and compatibility of hardware. The auditor is concerned that there is reasonable accountability for hardware, and that diverse hardware equipment does not affect compatibility with other pieces of hardware.

"Distributed systems" means distributed authority to select hardware designs made specifically for the hardware needs of an operating unit. However, "distributed hardware" does not mean standalone hardware. The equipment selected for a distributed system is a resource of the distributed system. While autonomy exists in satisfying needs of local users, the same cooperative spirit needed to make the distributed systems successful must also exist in hardware selection.

The hardware in each part of a distributed system is a system resource. These resources must be assignable to all users of the distributed system. "Assignable" may mean movement of physical hardware, or it may mean assigning the use of the resource to another unit of the distributed system.

The auditor should review the hardware of the distributed system from a perspective of accountability and compatibility. A checklist for auditing the distributed hardware concerns is provided in **Figure 4-7, Distributed Hardware Concerns.**

In completing the checklists in Figures 4-7 through 4-11 the auditor should evaluate the handling of the concern as **very adequate, adequate, indadequate,** or **not applicable.** The evaluations mean:

- **Very Adequate:** The implemented controls appear to satisfactorily solve all concerns in a very competent manner.

- **Adequate:** The implemented controls are such that any problems occurring as a result of the implementation will not significantly affect the operation.

- **Inadequate:** The concern has not been adequately addressed, or the solution will not eliminate the occurrence of significant problems.

- **Not Applicable (N/A):** The item of concern is not applicable to the installation being reviewed.

Figure 4-7

DISTRIBUTED HARDWARE CONCERNS

No.	Concern	Concern Evaluation				Comments
		Very Adequate	Adequate	Inadequate	N/A	
1.	Have the input data requirements been established?					
2.	Have provisions been made for backup hardware?					
3.	Has hardware performance criteria been established?					
4.	Does the small processor at the outlying units have the capability to utilize the capacity available to local users?					
5.	Have provisions been made for the hardware among the various units to interface properly?					
6.	Have plans been made to increase the capacity of the hardware if the need exists?					
7.	Are the hardware control features, such as memory protection, being utilized?					

For concern evaluations of **inadequate** or **adequate** where there is some question regarding the adequacy of implementation, the **comments** column should contain some explanation of the concern.

At the completion of the review, all concerns rated **inadequate** should be pursued, as should **adequate** evaluations where a note in the **comments** column indicated some special concern. The auditor should make a determination as to the seriousness of the item and take whatever action is required.

- **Distributed Processing Auditing Concerns**

Processing in a distributed system involves application programs, the operating system, and people operating equipment. The combination of the three utilizes the capabilities of the hardware to produce processing results.

In reviewing the processing area of a distributed system, the auditors need to satisfy themselves that the following concerns have been adequately addressed.

- Processing Capacity Is Adequate
- Processing Capacity Is Assignable
- People Are Adequately Trained
- Application Systems Produce Compatible Data
- Adequate Planning Exists For Continued Compatible Growth

Figure 4-8, Distributed Processing Concerns, provides a checklist of items of concern for distributed processing. In reviewing distributed processing, the auditor should evaluate these concerns in the same manner as outlined in Figure 4-7.

- **Distributed Data Auditing Concerns**

One of the major concerns of distributed systems is the distribution of data. In standalone systems, data existed in many units of the organization. However, in those instances, the data was not shared by multiple users. In a distributed system, data is shared.

With multiple physical databases, the need exists to have common elements in two or more physical databases. Having the same data appear in multiple databases increases the problem of data integrity. Detailed records must be maintained regarding every location of a particular data element. When a change is made in one physical database, it must be made to all databases containing that common data element.

Figure 4-8
(Page 1)

DISTRIBUTED PROCESSING CONCERNS

No.	Concern	Concern Evaluation				Comments
		Very Adequate	Adequate	Inadequate	N/A	
1.	Are there agreements between remote distributed processing sites on policies regarding receipt and transmission of communications between the sites?					
2.	Have provisions been made for restart and recovery in the event of system failure?					
3.	Have documented operating instructions been prepared?					
4.	Have documented operating instructions been distributed to all units?					
5.	Have operation personnel in all units been instructed on the operating requirements of the distributed system?					
6.	Is a message priority structure used to ensure that the most important messages get delivered first?					
7.	Is a processing priority structure used to ensure that the most important processing gets accomplished first?					
8.	Are all messages received by the remote distributed processing site logged for backup and audit trail purposes?					
9.	Is the processing documentation up-to-date?					

DISTRIBUTED PROCESSING CONCERNS

No.	Concern	Concern Evaluation				Comments
		Very Adequate	Adequate	Inadequate	N/A	
10.	Has provision been made for dynamic load leveling so that the total processing load can be distributed across available computers?					
11.	Can the load leveling procedures move the processing capability to the data?					
12.	Can the load leveling capabilities move the data to the processing capabilities?					
13.	Have procedures been developed to handle lock-out situations (i.e., user A has record one and is holding it until he gets record two, while user B has record two and is holding it until he gets record one).					
14.	Has a detailed plan been prepared outlining the requirements for the distributed data system?					
15.	Have processing performance criteria been established?					
16.	Have provisions been made for the software in the various units to interface properly?					
17.	Have the output processing requirements been established?					

In any database environment, there is the problem of multiple accesses to the same data element at the same time. A major operating problem in a single database is to lock out secondary accesses to a data element when it is in the process of being updated. Current technology with one database is still struggling with the solution to this problem. If the same element appears in multiple databases and can be accessed by many users simultaneously, the solution to the lockout problem is magnified.

Another data concern in a distributed environment is data definition. With distributed systems goes a high degree of autonomy. If one unit wants to slightly deviate the definition for their own needs, they may be able to do it. On the other hand, permitting this to happen can cause serious compatibility problems when consolidating data.

A checklist for reviewing the distributed data concerns is provided in **Figure 4-9, Distributed Data Concerns.** The auditors should satisfy themselves that these concerns have been adequately addressed in the distributed system. The checklist rating should be performed in accordance with instructions for Figure 4-7.

- **Distributed Control Auditing Concerns**

One of the least recognized concerns of a distributed system is the distribution of control. Studies of control in a data processing environment have previously indicated that too little attention has been paid to the subject of control in a computerized business environment. Thus, without learning how to fully control a conventional data processing environment, we are moving rapidly into a distributed data processing environment.

There are no standards by which to determine adequacy of controls in a distributed data processing environment. In existing distributed systems, there have not been enough true distributing systems experiencing control failures from which one could learn. It must be recognized that much of our experience in building adequate controls is obtained from failure to achieve adequacy of control in previous systems.

One of the major control problems in a distributed system is enforcement of standards. When processing units have a high degree of autonomy, issuance of standards from a central location is inconsistent with the distributed objectives. It is difficult to tell a local manager that the manager has authority over a computer operation, and then, at the same time, describe in detail how that operation is to be run.

Figure 4-10, Distributed Control Concerns, provides a checklist of items of concern regarding distributed control. This area is one in which the auditor can make the greatest contribution. The previous three areas are ones in which data processing personnel have a solid base on which to enter a new technology. The same is not true in control. The auditor should evaluate the control items in accordance with the instructions for Figure 4-7.

Figure 4-9

DISTRIBUTED DATA CONCERNS

No.	Concern	Concern Evaluation				Comments
		Very Adequate	Adequate	Inadequate	N/A	
1.	Is the data stored at one remote distributed processing site backed up in another remote site?					
2.	Does each message contain a code identifying the sender?					
3.	Does each message contain a code identifying the intended receiver of the message?					
4.	Is there a provision to store messages destined for a remote distributed processing site that is out of service?					
5.	Do the data rules prohibit any user from redefining data?					
6.	Could the data in the distributed databases be combined into a single organization-wide database should the need exist?					
7.	Are standard data definitions used in all units?					
8.	When common data elements need updating, has provision been made to update all duplicate data elements simultaneously?					
9.	Is the data documentation up-to-date?					
10.	Is one person accountable for each element of data?					

Figure 4-10
(Page 1)

DISTRIBUTED CONTROL CONCERNS

No.	Concern	Concern Evaluation				Comments
		Very Adequate	Adequate	Inadequate	N/A	
1.	Has a policy been established pertaining to what can and cannot be processed on a distributed data system?					
2.	Has a detailed plan been made for implementing a distributed data system?					
3.	Has a detailed schedule been established for implementing a distributed data system?					
4.	Do all the remote distributed processing sites get together on a regular basis to discuss operating procedures?					
5.	Is it forbidden to enter master commands in one remote distributed processing site for execution at another remote distributed processing site?					
6.	Has a detailed conversion plan been established for moving to a distributed data system?					
7.	Has a detailed plan been established to provide sufficient training for all people involved in a distributed data system?					
8.	Have the users established acceptance criteria that must be met before the distributed system goes operational?					
9.	Have procedures been established to monitor system response times?					

Figure 4-10
(Page 2)

DISTRIBUTED CONTROL CONCERNS

No.	Concern	Concern Evaluation				Comments
		Very Adequate	Adequate	Inadequate	N/A	
10.	Has provision been made to monitor the number of times, and the length of time, that system malfunctions occur?					
11.	Do all remote distributed processing sites prepare schedules of needs so that the allocation of resources can be equitably distributed?					
12.	Is the user at one remote distributed processing site forbidden from overriding the conventions at another remote distributed processing site?					
13.	Has one individual (or processing unit) been appointed to control the distributed processing system?					
14.	Is the individual in charge of the distributed processing system the only individual able to use system commands affecting more than one site?					
15.	Have the system commands affecting more than one site been restricted to one terminal?					
16.	Is the system monitored to determine that remote distributed processing sites participate as full partners in the distributed processing system?					
17.	Are reports maintained on the amount of resources used by each unit in the distributed processing system?					

Figure 4-10
(Page 3)

DISTRIBUTED CONTROL CONCERNS

No.	Concern	Concern Evaluation				Comments
		Very Adequate	Adequate	Inadequate	N/A	
18.	Have all users' needs in the distributed system been equally addressed?					
19.	Have cost/benefit analyses been made on the distributed processing concept?					
20.	Have post-implementation reviews been made to determine that installation specifications were achieved?					
21.	Does the failure of any one unit affect the continued operation of any other unit?					
22.	Were other alternatives considered before going to the distributed data systems concept?					
23.	Do all remote distributed processing sites obtain regularly scheduled maintenance?					
24.	Are outgoing messages verified that they contain a valid destination address?					
25.	Do the remote distributed processing sites send copies of control and problem reports to a central site for central review and action?					
26.	Has the insurance coverage been adjusted to reflect the increased resources at remote distributed processing sites?					

• Distributed Security Auditing Concerns

Organizations can develop a good security system for assets in a central location. This method has proven true in data processing. When we store our data in central locations, we only use remote facilities for retention of backup information. In a centralized environment, the people with the highest data processing skills are present to oversee security on a daily basis. This has made security an accomplishable task in EDP.

The use of communication lines added a new dimension to security. No longer was the computer room "vault" adequate. Information was passing in and out of the computer room over communication lines on a regular basis. It was now necessary to secure both the communication lines and the computer room.

The advent of distributed data processing systems brings distributed data, hardware, processing, and control. Security must now progress beyond what was expected in on-line applications. Just as we were learning how to secure information over communication lines, technology changes again. The use of cryptography, call-back techniques, and other communication control practices have proved to be effective controls for safeguarding data over communication lines. These, plus new controls, are needed in a distributed environment.

The adage, "Divide and Conquer," may prove a reality in distributed data processing systems. No longer can security be concentrated in a central location. As processing is distributed, so must security. It is not practical to build well-secured computer rooms in a distributed data processing system. One of the main characteristics of distributed systems is the ability to reassign resources. This reassignment can mean movement of hardware, processing, and control. One day, processing may be heavily concentrated at Location A, tomorrow Location B, and the next day Location C. This continually moving concentration of processing and data require mobile security.

A checklist of distributed security concerns is provided in **Figure 4-11, Distributed Security Concerns.** The auditor should evalute these concerns in accordance with the instructions for Figure 4-7.

At the completion of reviewing distributed security concerns, the auditor will have completed the distributed system review. The total review of the five areas must be consolidated to get an overview of the adequacy of control in the distributed system environment. The report on the review should be prepared in a manner similar to that of a review of the data center. It should be distributed to the appropriate parties.

Figure 4-11
(Page 1)

DISTRIBUTED SECURITY CONCERNS

No.	Concern	Concern Evaluation				Comments
		Very Adequate	Adequate	Inadequate	N/A	
1.	Where appropriate, have remote distributed processing sites been restricted to authorize applications for that site?					
2.	Has a user profile been established to restrict access to individuals authorized to use resources?					
3.	Are passwords used to identify users of the distributed systems?					
4.	Are remote distributed processing sites in a physically secure location so that only authorized personnel can actually use the equipment?					
5.	If lockable keyboards are a feature on the remote distributed processing terminals, is the feature properly utilized?					
6.	If sufficient unauthorized accesses are attempted from a remote distributed processing site to data at other sites, is that remote site locked out of the system?					
7.	Do terminals have a nonprinting feature for use when individuals enter their security passwords?					
8.	If the terminal cannot be contained in a physically secure location, has a physical keylock been put on the terminal's off/on switch?					

Figure 4-11
(Page 2)

DISTRIBUTED SECURITY CONCERNS

No.	Concern	Concern Evaluation: Very Adequate	Adequate	Inadequate	N/A	Comments
9.	Must the remote distributed processing site facilities be opened by a supervisor?					
10.	Are remote distributed processing sites locked out of the distributed systems during the hours when they are normally not in operation?					
11.	Is the concept of the callback technique (when a terminal calls over a common carrier communication line to another terminal, the second terminal disconnects the connection and calls back to the known location of the first terminal) used when sensitive data is involved?					
12.	If dial-up telephone numbers are used, are the numbers kept secret?					
13.	Have the objectives of security at the remote sites been documented?					
14.	Is security at all the remote distributed processing sites reviewed to ensure consistency in security procedures?					
15.	Are encryption or secret keys used to protect sensitive data?					
16.	Are control reports prepared on security violations (including unsuccessful attempts using passwords)?					

Figure 4-11
(Page 3)

DISTRIBUTED SECURITY CONCERNS

No.	Concern	Concern Evaluation				Comments
		Very Adequate	Adequate	Inadequate	N/A	
17.	Have disaster plans been developed?					
18.	Have disaster plans been tested?					
19.	Are there procedures on the preferred methods for disposal of sensitive documents at remote distributed processing sites?					
20.	Has a security classification been established for sensitive data?					
21.	Is the totality of all the data in the system considered when determining the data's security classification?					
22.	Is the documentation of security procedures up-to-date?					
23.	Are employees having access to sensitive data subject to special controls?					
24.	Are all systems commands logged so they can be reviewed by supervision at a later time?					
25.	Is there stringent control over the use and storage of circuit test equipment?					

4.3 AUDITING STANDALONE SMALL COMPUTER SYSTEMS

Many auditors audit a small computer site using the same approaches as when auditing large computers. Unfortunately, these approaches may identify control problems that are not correctable. For example, in a large computer installation, a control principle is "do not let programmers into the computer room or operate the computer." In a small computer installation, this is still a good control principle, but not a practical principle. The installation may only have two data processing individuals. One is a combination data processing manager/systems analyst and programmer. The other is a computer operator. When the computer operator is away, the programmer must operate the computer. There is no alternative.

The auditor cannot expect the small computer site to devote the same amount of resources to the development of control procedures that is expected of a large central computer organization. The auditor should not expect to find a standards manual, a detailed systems development control methodology, or a separate data library.

Situations which were considered low risk in the large computer site may constitute high risk in the small computer site. For example, the reliability of hardware and software is not as great in the small computer as in the large central computer. The large computer manufacturer can afford to spend the time and resources to develop redundant hardware circuits, adding controls, and debugging software that, if performed by the manufacturer of the small computer, may put them at a severe competitive price disadvantage.

The auditor needs to re-examine control and audit methods in the small computer. Auditors need to redirect their efforts to the risks in the small computer installation. The extensive control checklists that are available are not necessarily applicable.

4.4 SMALL COMPUTER SYSTEM CONTROL ISSUES

Control issues are threats to the integrity of the small computer system. These control issues can be used in establishing the scope of the audit. The issues define the areas of concern to the auditor.

The auditor selects those issues that are to be included in the audit. For example, one of the issues is user satisfaction. An audit may be financial oriented, and thus would not be concerned with the operational aspects of the small computer installation, such as user satisfaction. In another audit, however, the concern that users' needs are not being satisfied may be a major objective.

The auditor needs to understand the control issues in a small computer environment. Once this understanding has been gained, then the auditor determines the applicability of each control issue to the audit. The identification of the applicable control issues determines the small computer audit scope.

The small computer control issues are listed in **Figure 4-12, Small Computer System Audit and Control Issues,** and are described below:

1. **Systems Development Control Issue:**

   Many small installations do not take advantage of the time-tested techniques for developing systems properly. There is waste inherent in poor systems development. For example, it is far superior to follow the process in designing systems of defining requirements, developing system specifications, and then to do the programming and testing. In some small computer installations, users begin the system development process by writing programs. These factors are of management concern.

   The auditors' concern in the developmental process should be primarily directed toward the financial processing workload as versus one-time analytical systems. Those non-financial systems, with minimal control needs, do not require a highly structured systems development approach. The effort required to build well controlled financial systems is worthwhile.

2. **Systems Documentation Control Issue:**

   Purchased or developed small computer applications may only have minimal documentation. Users developing their own applications frequently feel they do not need documentation. The documentation provided by small computer vendors varies significantly from outstanding to poor. Some small computers have excellent, easy-to-read, easy-to-follow documentation, while others provide only the minimal documentation necessary. Lacking adequate documentation, users may not be able to use the system effectively or to modify applications economically.

3. **Hardware Reliability Control Issue:**

   Large computers have extensive redundant circuitry. The hardware is able to check on itself. For example, mathematical operations may be performed twice or more and the results compared to ensure the reliability of the calculation. The lower-cost small computers usually do not include the same type of reliability features.

   Many large computers have self-diagnosing circuitry. When problems occur, the computer diagnoses its own problem and takes action accordingly. Small computers without some of this diagnosis circuitry may encounter similar problems but, without the self-diagnosing circuitry to notify the operator, the problem is not detected.

4. **Software Reliability Control Issue:**

   Quality software requires extensive testing. Testing is a very costly process. Without this testing, software may occasionally fail or, even worse, produce erroneous results without detection.

Figure 4-12
(Page 1)

SMALL COMPUTER SYSTEM AUDIT AND CONTROL ISSUES

Item No.	Issue	Description
1.	Systems Development	The procedure to develop or acquire applications.
2.	Systems Documentation	The formal documentation available explaining what the system does and how it performs its function.
3.	Hardware Reliability	The ability of the hardware to process data based upon the hardware specifications.
4.	Software Reliability	The ability of the software to process data based upon the software specifications.
5.	Hardware Maintenance	The preventive and corrective program to ensure the continued reliability of hardware.
6.	Software Maintenance	The preventive and corrective program to ensure the continued operation of the software.
7.	Training	The materials and courses provided to explain how the hardware, software, and application systems function.
8.	Service Level	Assurance that the desired level of processing can be sustained.

Figure 4-12
(Page 2)

SMALL COMPUTER SYSTEM
AUDIT AND CONTROL ISSUES

Item No.	Issue	Description
9.	Standardization	Use of uniform procedures to increase the performance and ease of use in maintenance of the resources.
10.	Access Control	Procedures to prevent the unauthorized use of small computer resources.
11.	Recovery	The procedures and tools necessary to restore the operation after integrity has been lost.
12.	Audit Trails	The records required to reconstruct and substantiate processing.
13.	Cost-Effectiveness	The procedures to ensure that the small computer operations are beneficial to the organization.
14.	Controlled Applications Processing	The procedures and measures installed in application systems to ensure the accuracy, completeness, and authorization of data.
15.	Continuity of Operations	The ability to maintain operations to meet the needs of the organization.
16.	User Satisfaction	Meeting the established requirements of users.

Many small computer users rely heavily on vendor-produced system and application software. This reliance is necessary because of the lack of data processing knowledge by those individuals. Therefore, when software produces erroneous results, the users may not be able to detect the problem, or they may be uncertain of the cause and correction.

5. **Hardware Maintenance Control Issue:**

Any piece of machinery can fail. When it does, service is needed to restore the hardware to its normal condition. Vendors of small computers may or may not service their own computer. In addition, if they service the computer, they may not do it onsite. Some vendors may not even have local representatives and, thus, a user would be required to ship the computer back to the factory for repair. If the user only has one small computer, they can be left without computer capacity for a period of many days, weeks, or even months.

6. **Software Maintenance Control Issue:**

Software has the same type of problems as hardware. When problems occur, they need to be fixed. In some instances, the small computer user may have the source code of the software and, thus, have the opportunity to fix the problem. In other instances, the vendor refuses to release the source code, in which case the vendor must fix the software package.

When the small computer user relies upon a software package and it fails, they may need it fixed quickly. Small computer vendors may not have the staff to fix a software package in a reasonable period of time. In some instances, it may be difficult even to contact the vendor and explain the problem. Many small computer users have only minimal data processing skills and have a handicap in attempting to identify a problem and the potential cause of that problem.

7. **Training Control Issue:**

Users in a small computer installation need training in both the operation of the hardware and the software. Many small computer vendors offer no formal training. Those vendors may or may not supply self-study instructional material to help the user learn to use the hardware and software capabilities.

The scope and ease of understanding of these training tools may determine how effectively the small computer can be utilized. Poorly explained features may never be used. In addition, users may spend large amounts of time attempting to learn how to use the small computer because inadequate training material is available to them. Also, changes and modifications to hardware and software may have no training material accompanying them.

8. **Service Level Control Issue:**

Small computers can easily become overloaded. A small computer that works well with one or two users may flounder when additional users are added. Their capacity is limited. When the capacity of the system is approached, the service level degrades quickly.

Some hardware commands and software capabilities may be inefficient. For example, some of the mathematical functions may take an extensive amount of time to execute. If the users are unaware of these inefficiencies, they may use capabilities which require an unreasonable amount of time for execution.

9. **Standardization Control Issue:**

Standards should exist within a single small computer environment and between small computer environments in an organization. While it is recognized that a small computer installation cannot afford the expenditure of large amounts of resources to develop standards, some minimal standards should be established. For example, access standards should be established.

The long-range direction for small computers is to become connected into a network. Without some long-range planning, organizations may acquire various small computers which are not compatible. When this happens, data from one computer cannot be readily transmitted or transferred to another computer.

10. **Access Control Issue:**

Access control is the key control in the small computer environment. Restricting usage of the small computer resources is the strongest control that can be used. Access controls need to limit access to the physical computer area as well as to the programs and data.

Physical access controls can be difficult to install in a small computer environment. Low-cost, workable alternatives to a secure computer room are available, however. The terminal can be located near a supervisor's desk, so that person can control physical access to the computer. Another effective method is to make one individual responsible for protecting the computer from unauthorized access.

Restricting access to programs and data may be dependent upon the capabilities built into the small computer operating system. Some small computers have a password system which restricts access to those people possessing the correct passwords. Although this is normally a single-level control, it is better than no control at all. Access also needs to be restricted to data stored off-site. Organizations store backup data away from the computer to protect the small computer site from a disaster. Should fire or other problems occur, the backup data permits the installation to regain operational status quickly.

11. **Recovery Control Issue:**

Recovery is restoring the integrity of computer processing after it has been lost. The data integrity can be lost due to hardware failure, software failure, application system failure, operator error, or physical catastrophe. The problem may come quickly, resulting in a halt to computer operations, or erroneous processing may occur for an extended period of time before it is uncovered.

Recovery is a two-part process. The first part is retaining the necessary data and developing the procedures necessary to recovery after a problem. The second part is executing those procedures when required.

Many small computer operating systems offer limited or no recovery procedures. This can be a problem if the small computer has large amounts of data stored on-line. In addition, many computers with only a single fixed drive may not have the capability to create backup data, and thus may have to recover by again manually entering the data.

The recovery process is one in which many small computer installations are deficient. Most recovery procedures are learned the hard way. The time and effort needed to develop a good recovery procedure is normally time well spent.

12. **Audit Trail Control Issue:**

Audit trails provide for the reconstruction of single-transaction processing and for the reprocessing of large amounts of data for recovery purposes. Audit trails can be created by the operating system or by application programming.

Large computer installations have operator logs, communication logs, and database system logs. These provide an excellent audit trail for backup and reconstruction purposes. Unfortunately, most small computer installations do not have these types of logs.

The need for an audit trail may not be obvious to the small computer installation. Many do not have accountants as consultants and, thus, do not recognize the significant role of the audit trail. This, coupled with the minimal or no audit trail aids provided by the vendor, can lead to some serious small computer processing reconstruction problems.

13. **Cost-Effectiveness Control Issue:**

Small computer systems should be installed because they are more cost-effective than other processing solutions. The determination of this cost-effectiveness requires the organization to determine or estimate both the benefits and the costs of installing a small computer. These cost/benefits can then be compared to other processing solutions.

Few small computer installations go through a detailed cost/benefit analysis. The reason for this is that the cost of the small computer usually does not warrant an extended study. When all of the costs are accumulated, however, organizations may be surprised at the total costs associated with obtaining a small computer.

Many organizations estimate that it costs three or four times the cost of the small computer to prepare for the installation. These other costs include evaluation and selection of the computers, the contractual process, training of employees to use the computer, site preparation, obtaining additional disks, paper, etc. After these costs have been expended, additional funds are necessary to obtain or develop application systems.

Small computer installations need not go through the same detailed cost analysis performed by the large computer installation. They should perform a cost/benefit calculation, however. Without this calculation, many noncost-effective installations may be installed.

14. Controlled Applications Processing Issue:

One of the major issues is the control within applications processing. Controls are necessary to ensure that transaction processing is accurate, complete, and authorized. Without adequate controls, the integrity of processing cannot be assured.

Control in an application begins when the data is entered. Control assures accuracy of input and processing, integrity of data files, and accuracy and completeness of output reports. In addition, control should prevent improper transactions from being processed.

Controls in financial applications should balance the computer data to externally-controlled control totals. These external controls provide assurance that the data within the computerized application is adequately controlled. For example, in accounts receivable, the cash applied to the receivables should be reconciled to the cash deposited in the bank.

15. Continuity of Operation Control Issue:

The small computer installation should determine the importance of continuity of operation. Management should decide the number of hours, minutes, or days that the computer can be down without adversely impacting their operations. This is the primary decision in determining the procedures installed to ensure continuity of operation.

The small computer issues included in this section describe the types of risks faced. Any one of these risks could cause the computer to go down and not be operational for extended periods of time. Once the maximum down period has been determined, the necessary countermeasures can be designed to ensure that operations can continue.

In small computer installations, it may be necessary to have two or more computers to ensure continuity of operation. However, this may only be effective against hardware failures and not effective against some of the other risks. The importance of continuity of operation determines the amount of resources expended to ensure that those operations continue.

16. **User Satisfaction Control Issue:**

User satisfaction in a small computer installation may be difficult to measure. If users are skilled, and computer requirements are established in enough detail so that they can be measurable, then user satisfaction can be measured. In many small computer installations, however, user expectations have not been defined and, thus, are not measurable.

Prior to approving the acquisition of a small computer system, the expectations for that computer should be defined and quantified. The results can then be measured against the requirements to determine achievement. In addition, users should be queried as to whether or not they are achieving their objectives because requirements change. This may make measurements against initial requirements inappropriate.

4.5 SMALL COMPUTER SYSTEM AUDIT APPROACH

The small computer system audit process presented here provides a step-by-step procedure for auditing a small computer installation. The method is similar to that used for any audit situation but is customized for the small computer installation. This section describes the small computer audit process, and the remaining parts describe how to execute those audit process steps.

The small computer audit process involves the following five steps:

Step 1: Determine Small Computer System Use

Step 2: Identify Control Issues

Step 3: Identify Internal Control Weaknesses

Step 4: Design and Execute Audit Tests

Step 5: Develop Opinion and Write Report

STEP 1: Determine Small Computer System Use

Small computer systems can be used for standalone operation or distributed processing. In evaluating a small computer installation, the auditor must first determine which use is being made of the computer. Although a small computer system may be used for more than one use, the auditor should determine the dominant use.

The audit process described in this section is for use with standalone small computers. If the small computer is part of a distributed network, the auditor should refer to Section 4.2, which discusses the audit process in a distributed system.

STEP 2: Identify Control Issues

Use of the small computer poses risks to the organization. These risks can be described as control issues. Sixteen control issues have been described in this section. The auditor must determine which of those issues are enough of a threat to require an audit review. If the auditor determines that a control issue, such as hardware maintenance, is not an issue in the organization, then no additional auditing need take place for that potential concern. However, if the auditor determines that hardware maintenance is a control issue that needs to be addressed, then it should be included in the audit program.

STEP 3: Identify Internal Control Weaknesses

The auditor must determine whether internal controls are adequate for those control issues included within the audit program. If control weaknesses are detected, then additional auditing must take place to determine whether or not that control weakness is resulting in a loss to the organization. Checklists are provided to review the adequacy of controls (Figures 4-13 through 4-28).

STEP 4: Design and Execute Audit Tests

The auditor conducts tests for two purposes: first, to determine if the identified controls are in place and working; and second, to determine the extent of losses associated with identified control weaknesses. Some of the more common small computer audit tools and techniques are described.

STEP 5: Develop Opinion and Write Report

The last part of the audit process is to develop an opinion on the adequacy of control and to communicate that opinion to management. Tips and techniques on writing reports for the small computer system environment are provided.

- **Reviewing Small Computer System Controls**

The system of internal controls should be reviewed periodically. As stated previously, the small computer controls will be different than the controls in the large computer installation. The controls reviewed are those designed to reduce risks inherent in the previously discussed control issues.

Segregation of duties is difficult in a small computer system installation. The segregation among operations achievable in a large installation is not achievable in a small installation due to the small size of staff. Thus, auditors cannot rely heavily upon segregation of duties for control in a small computer system installation. The auditor must rely on other controls and tests in determining the integrity of operations. They may be required to conduct more tests in a small computer installation because of this inability to rely on a weak system of internal controls.

The type of controls that an auditor might find in lieu of segregation of duties include:

- Supervisory Review
- More Extensive Application Controls
- More Independently-Maintained Control Totals Outside of the Computer Area
- More Frequent Audits
- Mandatory Vacations
- Requiring Two People to Be Present Whenever the Computer Is in Operation

Internal control checklists in this section have been designed for each of the small computer control issues. The auditor determines which issues are to be reviewed during the audit and selects the checklist for that control issue.

The issues divide the small computer system installation into controllable units. Therefore, the issues can be evaluated individually. There is one checklist for each of the sixteen small computer control issues.

The checklists are designed to be answered "yes" or "no." A "yes" answer indicates the item of concern has been adequately addressed by the small computer installation. A "no" answer indicates that further investigation should be undertaken to determine the severity of the concern. A "not applicable" (N/A) column is provided for those items included on the checklist which are not applicable for the organization being reviewed. A "comments" column is provided to qualify "yes" answers in which a concern is not completely satisfied, and to amplify "no" areas. Comments are helpful in conducting an investigation of the item.

The auditor must use more discretion in reviewing controls in a small computer system installation. The auditor should not expect, nor recommend, the same level of control as exists in a large installation. That level of control would not be cost-effective in a small computer installation and may, in fact, make the small computer installation unworkable.

The questions in the following checklists must also be tempered by cost-effectiveness criteria. The one- or two-person small computer system installation will have fewer controls than the one staffed by ten or twenty people, and so on. The auditor must take into account the size of the staff as well as the size of the small computer.

The level of controls is also dependent upon the importance of the application to the organization. Those less important applications will have less documentation, less controls, etc. The auditor must also temper the internal control assessment by the importance of the application to the organization.

The checklists included are:

Figure 4-13: **Systems Development Control**

Figure 4-14: **Systems Documentation Control**

Figure 4-15: **Hardware Reliability Control**

Figure 4-16: **Software Reliability Control**

Figure 4-17: **Hardware Maintenance Control**

Figure 4-18: **Software Maintenance Control**

Figure 4-19: **Training Control**

Figure 4-20: **Service Level Control**

Figure 4-21: **Standardization Control**

Figure 4-22: **Access Control**

Figure 4-23: **Recovery Control**

Figure 4-24: **Audit Trail Control**

Figure 4-25: **Cost-Effectiveness Control**

Figure 4-26: **Controlled Applications Processing**

Figure 4-27: **Continuity of Operations Control**

Figure 4-28: **User Satisfaction Control**

Figure 4-13

SYSTEMS DEVELOPMENT CONTROL

No.	Item	Response			
		Yes	No	N/A	Comments
1.	Has an approval procedure been established so that management can approve applications before they are started?				
2.	Has an approval procedure been established requiring management approval prior to purchasing computer applications?				
3.	Is the cost/benefit of an application determined prior to commencing the project?				
4.	Is a determination made if an application can be purchased prior to developing an application inhouse?				
5.	Before placing it on the small computer system, is a determination made that the computer has sufficient capacity to execute the desired function?				
6.	Prior to approving the project, has it been determined if the proposed small computer system application can be performed by another application system in the organization?				
7.	Do small computer personnel possess the necessary skills to develop applications for the small computer?				
8.	Has a systems development procedure been established?				
9.	If so, is the complexity of the process related to the importance of the project?				

SYSTEMS DOCUMENTATION CONTROL

No.	Item	Response			
		Yes	No	N/A	Comments
1.	Has a minimum level of documentation for small computer application systems been established?				
2.	Is a minimum level of documentation applied to purchased applications?				
3.	Are operator instructions documented?				
4.	Does documentation exist on how to use the outputs from the application?				
5.	Is there documentation on how to fix a problem in purchased applications?				
6.	Do purchased applications have documentation explaining how to get vendor help?				
7.	Are the application controls documented?				
8.	Is documentation prepared in accordance with the importance of the application to the organization?				

HARDWARE RELIABILITY CONTROL

No.	Item	Responses			
		Yes	No	N/A	Comments
1.	Does the vendor provide a guaranteee on the reliability of the hardware?				
2.	Does the hardware have circuitry to identify hardware problems to the operator?				
3.	Is the organization provided with a manual explaining how to test the reliability of the hardware circuitry?				
4.	Is a log maintained of hardware errors to help track the reliability of the hardware?				
5.	Are procedures established to contact the vendor in the event of hardware problems?				
6.	Is the reliability history of the small computer system evaluated prior to purchase through reference to publications or a survey of existing users?				

Figure 4-16

SOFTWARE RELIABILITY CONTROL

No.	Item	Response			
		Yes	No	N/A	Comments
1.	Has the degree of reliability desired in the software been determined?				
2.	Have tests been made to determine that the software achieves the predetermined degree of reliability?				
3.	Prior to purchase, have other users of purchased software been contacted to determine the reliability of the software?				
4.	If versions are changed, have backup versions been maintained in case the updated version proves unreliable?				
5.	Do the developers of the in-house software have the necessary skills to develop software?				
6.	Are procedures established on how to test software?				
7	Are logs maintained on software problems to identify high-problem softwa. ?				
8.	Are procedures established on vendor or developer contract to cope with software problems?				

HARDWARE MAINTENANCE CONTROL

No.	Item	Response			
		Yes	No	N/A	Comments
1.	Does the vendor of the hardware offer maintenance service?				
2.	Is the service convenient to obtain?				
3.	Has the maximum permissible downtime been established?				
4.	Can the vendor provide service within the maximum downtime?				
5.	Have procedures been developed on when and how to call vendor maintenance personnel?				
6.	Are small computer system operators trained in how to perform routine maintenance?				
7.	Has the cost of maintenance been predetermined and budgeted?				
8.	Are logs maintained to show the amount of downtime?				
9.	If downtime is excessive, can a refund or renegotiation of the contract be made with the vendor?				
10.	Are third-party services for maintenance available?				

SOFTWARE MAINTENANCE CONTROL

No.	Item	Response: Yes	No	N/A	Comments
1.	Does the installation possess the necessary skills to maintain in-house developed software?				
2.	Has a procedure been developed to indicate when maintenance should be performed?				
3.	Do the vendors of purchased software provide maintenance?				
4.	Is vendor maintenance convenient to obtain?				
5.	Has the cost of maintenance been determined?				
6.	Has the maximum desired downtime for software been determined?				
7.	Can the vendor provide maintenance within that downtime period?				
8.	Are logs maintained to show the amount of downtime?				
9.	If downtime is excessive, can a refund or a renegotiation of the contract be made with the vendor?				
10.	If the vendor goes out of business, is source code available for continuing modification of leased software packages?				
11.	If software package vendor goes out of business, are rights of user protected?				

Figure 4-19

TRAINING CONTROL

No.	Item	Response			
		Yes	No	N/A	Comments
1.	Does the vendor provide training classes on how to use the small computer system?				
2.	Are self-teach training materials available on the use of the small computer system?				
3.	Are training courses and/or training material available on purchased software application packages?				
4.	Are methods established to train users on in-house developed applications?				
5.	If a vendor goes out of business, does the organization own the rights to continue using the teaching courses?				
6.	If the vendor goes out of business, can the organization reproduce copyrighted materials for in-house use?				
7.	Are training materials updated when hardware, software, and in-house developed applications are updated?				
8.	Is the effort expended on training proportionate to the value of the resource to the organization?				

SERVICE LEVEL CONTROL

No.	Item	Response			
		Yes	No	N/A	Comments
1.	Are the resources adequate to handle the essential applications?				
2.	Has a procedure been established for prioritizing work when demand exceeds capacity?				
3.	Has a procedure been established for prioritizing work after a computer problem?				
4.	Has a procedure been established to prevent users from monopolizing resources?				
5.	Are service levels monitored to determine when action on the system capacity needs to be taken?				
6.	Have procedures been established to determine what new capacity requirements will be placed on the minicomputer?				
7.	Is a log of jobs maintained to determine where resources are utilized?				
8.	Does a long-range capacity plan exist?				
9.	Are users regularly queried as to their level of satisfaction?				

Figure 4-21

STANDARDIZATION CONTROL

No.	Item	Response			
		Yes	No	N/A	Comments
1.	Does the organization have a procedure to follow in acquiring small computer hardware and software?				
2.	Can all the organization's small computers communicate on the available network?				
3.	Are there certain vendor requirements, such as offering a language like BASIC, that must be met prior to acquiring a small computer system from that vendor?				
4.	Before it can become operational, does the small computer installation require operational programs to meet minimal standards such as preventing one program from destroying the data of another program?				
5.	Are data files adequately labeled so that they can be identified by an application program prior to use?				
6.	Has one individual been appointed to oversee the small computer standards?				

Figure 4-22

ACCESS CONTROL

No.	Item	Response			
		Yes	No	N/A	Comments
1.	Does the small computer operating software include access control?				
2.	Are procedures established to evaluate the access control features provided by the hardware and software vendors to determine whether or not they should be utilized?				
3.	Is a determination made for both data and programs as to who can have access to those resources?				
4.	Has a determination been made and enforced regarding who can have access to the small computer system facility?				
5.	Are small computer system access violations reported to management?				
6.	Have all the physical security measures been taken which can economically be utilized?				
7.	Are operators, systems programmers, and other small computer data processing personnel subject to the same access rules as any other user of the system?				

RECOVERY CONTROL

No.	Item	Response			
		Yes	No	N/A	Comments
1.	Has a determination been made regarding which applications need to be recovered after a problem?				
2.	Has a determination been made regarding how quickly each application must be recovered?				
3.	Are resources available to meet the above time constraints?				
4.	Has sufficient backup data been saved to meet the above requirements and time constraints?				
5.	Have recovery procedures been established?				
6.	Have recovery procedures been practiced to determine if they are effective?				
7.	Are operating personnel trained in recovery procedures?				
8.	Are recovery procedures documented?				
9.	Have arrangements been made for alternate processing, such as at another minicomputer site, in the event the minicomputer should be down for an extended period of time?				

Figure 4-24

AUDIT TRAIL CONTROL

No.	Item	Response			
		Yes	No	N/A	Comments
1.	Have audit trail requirements been defined for each application?				
2.	Can all financial transactions be traced to their appropriate control totals?				
3.	Can financial control totals be traced downward to all the supporting transactions?				
4.	Have the important transactions been identified?				
5.	Can important transactions be reconstructed if necessary?				
6.	Are procedures established to log operator actions?				
7.	Are procedures established to reconstruct programs if necessary?				
8.	In a communication environment, are procedures established to reconstruct communication processing if necessary?				
9.	In a database environment, have procedures been established to reconstruct database processing if necessary?				
10.	Is the audit trail information sufficient to support the reconstruction of processing and requirements?				

COST-EFFECTIVENESS CONTROL

No.	Item	Response			
		Yes	No	N/A	Comments
1.	Does management require a cost/benefit study prior to acquiring a small computer system?				
2.	If so, have those procedures been complied with?				
3.	Do the costs include documentation, training, site preparation, and other costs associated with installing a small computer?				
4.	Is a cost/benefit study made, even if analyzed in a cursory manner, prior to purchasing or installing new applications?				
5.	Are users of the small computer system aware of the costs associated with using that equipment?				
6.	Are small computer users aware of the cost of alternate means of processing?				
7.	Are system applications and reports regularly reviewed to ensure that unneeded or obsolete systems or reports are eliminated?				

CONTROLLED APPLICATIONS PROCESSING

No.	Item	Response			
		Yes	No	N/A	Comments
1.	Are the controlled risks identified?				
2.	Has the severity of those risks for the small computer applications been determined?				
3.	Are controls established to reduce the risks to an agreed upon level?				
4.	Are control violations documented and reported to management?				
5.	Does management take appropriate action on those control violations?				
6.	Are the controls documented?				
7.	Are the controls in the operating environment studied before building application controls?				
8.	Are the controls in purchased applications known?				
9.	Are the controls in purchased applications adequate?				
10.	If controls in purchased applications are inadequate, have steps been taken to supplement those controls?				

CONTINUITY OF OPERATIONS CONTROL

No.	Item	Response			
		Yes	No	N/A	Comments
1.	Have the operations needed for conducting the day-to-day work of the organization been identified?				
2.	Have procedures been established to ensure that those operations can be run on a timely basis?				
3.	Has sufficient data been stored off-site to ensure continuity of those operations in the event of a disaster?				
4.	Has sufficient documentation about the small computer operation been stored off-site so that processing can be continued in the event of a disaster?				
5.	Has a contingency plan been developed to restore operations in the event of a disaster?				
6.	Has the impact of disaster been identified, and sufficient countermeasures incorporated into the contingency plan to offset that impact?				

USER SATISFACTION CONTROL

No.	Item	Response			
		Yes	No	N/A	Comments
1.	Have the user's requirements been identified and documented?				
2.	Are those requirements measurable?				
3.	Have they been measured?				
4.	Have procedures been established to determine whether or not user requirements have been achieved?				
5.	As user requirements are changed, are the methods of measuring user satisfaction changed accordingly?				
6.	Are users periodically interviewed regarding whether or not the computer satisfies their needs?				
7.	Are procedures established to eliminate or change those systems which do not satisfy user needs?				

4.6 SMALL COMPUTER SYSTEM AUDIT TESTING

The auditor tests for one of the following four reasons:

1. To Evaluate the Functioning of Controls

2. To Identify Control Weaknesses

3. To Determine the Severity of the Control Weaknesses

4. To Substantiate Financial Balance

The control environment in a small computer installation may or may not allow the auditor to rely upon internal control. The auditor may review the system of control and make the decision that, because of the limited staff, duplication of duties, and the ready access of information to many people, the controls cannot be relied upon. In those instances, the auditor will make a decision to perform substantive testing. In other words, the auditor must verify the data in total that is processed by the small computer system.

If the auditor decides that some, or all, of the system of internal control may be reliable, then control testing can occur. Obviously, this is the more effective audit approach as lesser amounts of data need to be examined.

Audit testing in a small computer system can be divided into two general categories: testing when controls are unreliable; and testing when some reliance can be placed upon controls.

The type of tools and techniques used by the auditor to conduct tests will vary depending upon the category of the audit testing.

• Testing When Controls Are Unreliable

The size of the small computer system, the segregation of duties among the small computer staff, and the type of applications run on the computer affect the auditor's decision to rely or not to rely upon controls. When the auditor determines that controls are unreliable, then the auditor must concentrate audit tests on the data processed by the computer as opposed to the controls in place in the organization. The audit emphasis in this situation will be upon the existence of the items recorded by the computer.

Many auditors approach a small computer installation whose controls are unreliable as if it were a manual environment. They ignore the fact that a computer exists and base their audit upon the more traditional evidence. Providing traditional hard-copy evidence is available, which it is in many small computer installations, the auditor can perform an effective substantive audit while ignoring the computer.

Small computer installations without the traditional forms of evidence pose a dilemma to the auditor. When electronic evidence is the only evidence available, the auditor will have to request or obtain listings of that evidence. It would be more appropriate for the auditor to control and execute the programs that list the electronic evidence than ask the computer operators to perform the task for them. A question of auditor negligence may arise should the auditor opt to audit electronic evidence but not take the steps necessary to evaluate the population of evidence stored in the computer files.

The small computer system substantive audit begins by obtaining statements showing the data processed by the computer. The content of the statements will reflect the systems processed by the computer. For example, if financial data is processed, then financial statements will be produced.

The methods of audit to be used are similar to those used in any other audit of data. If the auditor needs to analyze and list the data on the computer files, it can be accomplished by using one of the following three methods:

a. **Audit Software:** Some audit software is available for small computers. In many instances, however, the software must be developed by the organization itself. The audit software is primarily used to list the evidence included in the data files.

b. **Small Computer Utility Programs:** Most small computers provide utility programs to perform a variety of tasks. For example, many IBM computers have the utility called Disk File Utility (DFU). This utility provides the capability of listing information contained on the computer disk files. The capabilities, with the exception of sampling, are similar to those in conventional audit software packages.

c. **Special Programming:** The auditor can use one of the languages available on the small computer to list the files used by that computer. One of the simpler languages included on many computers is BASIC. This language has capabilities similar to audit software, with the exception of sampling. With data auditing, the auditor normally wants to list all of the file as opposed to sampling from that file.

- **Evaluating Small Computer System Internal Controls**

When the auditor has made a decision that some reliance can be placed on small computer controls, then those controls must be tested.

The recommended assessment approach is for the auditor to evaluate controls based upon the small computer control issues described in this section. Rarely will the auditor be able to rely upon internal control for all the issues in a small computer installation but may be able to rely upon those controls dealing with certain issues. Many of these issues are operational as opposed to financial and, thus, are more internal audit than external audit oriented issues. For example, the internal auditor would be concerned with recovery and, even in a one-person computer installation, the auditor can assess the adequacy of recovery controls. These are normally not people dependent but procedural dependent.

With a limited data processing staff, it may be difficult to assess the reliability of controls that are dependent upon appropriate segregation of people. It may be necessary for the auditor to first assess the severity of the risk before testing the controls. If the risk is minimal, the auditor may not expect or require strong controls. On the other hand, if the risk is large, the auditor may look for strong controls. Both the auditor's test and the recommendations made to management should be based upon the severity of the risk.

The recommended testing approach in a small computer system environment will be based on whether the auditor is testing procedures or the segregation of functions. Both the approach and the testing will vary. Each audit situation is discussed individually.

- **Testing Segregation of Function Controls**

The small computer system control issues that involve the testing of segregation of function are:

1. Access Control
2. Audit Trails
3. Controlled Applications

The types of testing tools that are effective in evaluating the adequacy of control over these control issues include:

a. **Internal Control Questionnaire:** The use of an internal control questionnaire designed exclusively for the small computer environment helps assess the adequacy of controls in the environment. Note again that internal control questionnaires designed for large computer installations probably are not effective in a small computer environment. These small computer internal control checklists should be used as a guide to identify areas for audit probing. They should not be considered complete. The auditor may need to supplement the questionnaires based upon responses to questions and areas that are organizational dependent.

b. **Control Violations Testing:** The auditor attempts to accomplish a task by violating the control. For example, if the auditor should not be granted access to a particular resource, the auditor will attempt to obtain that resource to determine whether or not the controls are effective. Control violation tests can be used to test access controls, security procedures, and physical controls.

c. **Data File Analysis:** Using audit software or small computer utilities, the auditor performs an analysis of the computer data. The analysis is performed using audit software and can be a static analysis on data, provide a trend analysis, do comparisons between two files, etc. The auditor is probing, looking for weaknesses in control.

d. Documentation Reviews: The auditor reviews documentation to determine if controls are adequate for the desired purpose. For example, in determining if internal controls are adequate in purchased applications, the auditor would review the documentation provided by the vendor to determine whether or not the package contained sufficient controls. Documentation reviews can be time-consuming in that the auditor must learn what the application attempts to accomplish, how the application achieves those objectives, and then whether or not the documented controls satisfy the requirement under review.

e. Interview: The auditor discusses with one or more individuals an area of audit concern. For example, rather than review documentation to determine whether or not an application is adequately controlled, the auditor may interview the individual responsible for that application. The auditor would ask that individual the same questions that the auditor hopes to answer through a documentation review. However, the auditor should be cautioned that people tend to explain things as they should be happening rather than how they may, in fact, be happening.

f. Manual Auditing: The auditor uses those tools and techniques effective in a manual audit. This would include vouching, confirmation, and refooting mathematical information. While these procedures do not utilize the power of the computer or address some of the more sophisticated methods of control, they may be effective in a small computer system environment in which an adequate audit trail exists, and where there is only minimal reliance on electronic evidence and automated controls.

- **Testing Procedures**

Testing of procedures will evaluate the small computer system control issues described in Figures 4-13 to 4-28.

The procedural testing relies less heavily on the people-oriented controls and more heavily on the development, implementation, and operation of good methods and procedures of doing work. Thus, the computer with no staff, or a very small data processing staff, can still be reviewed for the adequacy of their procedures.

In addition to the effective testing techniques and procedures described for testing segregation of functions, the following testing tools can be used:

a. <u>Authoritative Source:</u> The auditor may wish to consult with an authoritative source regarding some aspect of control. For example, if the auditor was concerned about hardware maintenance or hardware reliability, the auditor may wish to refer to some of the updating services which evaluate hardware and software. In other instances, they should refer to FTP Manuals, which outline good methods and procedures for performing data processing procedures.

b. <u>Disaster Testing:</u> The auditor simulates a disaster to determine if the organization can recoup from that disaster. The type of disasters tested can include hardware disasters, operating system disasters, and application system disasters. Normally, the auditor picks a small area and asks the installation manager to recoup without using the on-site documentation, programs, hardware, and data.

c. <u>Observation and Investigation:</u> The auditor may wish to observe and investigate the execution of procedures. Knowing what the procedures are may not determine how those procedures are practiced in the computer installation. Observing and investigating situations to determine that the appropriate procedures were used and are effective will provide the auditor with assurance as to whether or not the procedural controls function properly.

d. <u>Benchmarking:</u> The auditor may wish to establish, or have users establish, standards of performance. The auditor uses these standards to determine whether the procedures achieve the required or desired level of performance. The actual results are then measured against those benchmark standards. Failure to meet those standards indicates ineffective procedural controls.

4.7 DEVELOPING OPINION AND WRITING REPORT

The last step in a small computer system audit is to present to management the audit findings and recommendations. Management relies upon the experience and judgment of the auditor to develop those opinions and recommendations. This part of the process cannot be automated, nor does management want that process to be automated. Because auditing a small computer installation is different than auditing a large computer installation, however, the inclusion of a few tips and techniques on opinions and recommendations appears worthwhile.

In drawing conclusions and recommendations about a small computer system installation, the auditor should:

- **Think Small Computer:**

  The same type of conclusions and recommendations that may receive good acceptance in a large computer installation may be viewed as impractical and unworkable in a small computer installation. The auditor must place himself/herself in the position of small computer management, and then try to evaluate potential conclusions or recommendations to determine if they are meaningful to that installation. For example, the recognition that duties cannot be segregated the same way they are in a large computer installation is of no value to the small computer manager.

- **Subject Recommendations to a Cost-Effective Analysis:**

  The auditor should go through a mini cost/benefit calculation for each recommendation. If the auditor cannot convince himself/herself that the recommendation is cost-effective, it should not be made. If the idea is not cost-effective, the auditor may wish to consider other alternative recommendations that are more appropriate in a small computer environment.

- **Be Future Oriented:**

  The installation of a small computer system is normally the first step in a process that evolves and gets larger over a period of time. The auditor should put findings, conclusions, and recommendations in the context of what that installation might be a month, year, or two years from now. Using this line of thinking, some problems which may appear borderline in today's environment could conceivably be very serious as the installation grows. Unless the auditor takes this into account, some of the recommendations may not be presented in the proper context.

- **Write Small Reports:**

  Audit managers in small computer system installations do not want extensive audit reports. The installation may be a small responsibility for some managers, and to get a twenty- to thirty-page audit report will create an immediate negative impression. Audit reports in small computer installations should be presented in two to three pages. If more information is required, it can be presented as an appendix or a supplemental letter.

SECTION 5

SYSTEMS AND SOFTWARE CONSIDERATIONS

SECTION OVERVIEW

The ultimate success of a small business computer installation will depend less upon the particular hardware selected than upon the operating systems that are available and the quality of the application software. Hardware systems have many differences, and their careful selection is important, but software systems come in a vast variety of functions, languages, efficiencies, and controls. Hardware bugs may be found by electronic testing. Software bugs can only be found by the astute use of test data, and considerable operational experience. It is, therefore, imperative that particular attention be paid to the planning and operational management of the operating and application software. The following checklists are useful in planning the effort of system implementation or for reviewing the work that has been done on the software systems:

5.1 OPERATING SOFTWARE

Operating system software is one of the major advantages of large computer systems since it helps provide greatly increased functionality of the systems, with close control over the operation at the same time. The cost is, of course, a considerable overhead requirement and includes the need to have several competent technical persons on the staff who work full time on the system. With small computer systems, one alternative is to have minimal operating software and no technical support staff, relying completely on the vendor. This alternative should be unacceptable for any business, analytical, or technical work, on a small computer system in which more than one application system is being run, and where there is some requirement for management and audit control of the operation. The better alternative for small systems is to decide what level of operating system will give:

a. the needed system development and productivity support;

b. the needed data management and transaction processing facilities;

c. adequate resource management and security programs; and

d. adequate control features.

There are a wide variety of offerings in these areas, and the decision will have to be made based on the functional requirements that were determined for the particular applications involved. Some small computer systems offer operating system software that is remarkably similar to that for the larger computers in approach, but have fewer features and commands, and require much less technical support.

A very small operation can reasonably select capable system software, learn enough about it to know when problems have arisen, and rely on the vendor's personnel for technical support. The majority of small computer systems should have at least one person available locally who has been trained in the system software and can readily use system utilities and perform systems generations. In larger organizations, there should be experienced technical persons available who can readily handle any aspect of the required technical support.

Figure 5-1, Operating Software, is a checklist that covers the principal types of software which should be considered in planning a computer installation. The final selection of the software will depend upon the application system and operational requirements.

5.2 APPLICATION SOFTWARE - EVALUATION AND TESTING

The system vendor may give considerable aid in software testing, but the final responsibility rests with the purchaser's technical personnel and users. They must understand that they are signing off for a considerable investment, and that the vendors' prime interest is their own profits.

The test plan should have been established at the time of the definition of functional requirements, and refined when it was known which software was selected or developed. The test data should have been assembled by the original systems analysts

OPERATING SOFTWARE

No.	Item	Response			
		Yes	No	N/A	Comments
1.	Is there an Operating System in the computer which includes: a. an interactive system generator? b. a command language, both batch and interactive? c. HELP or other assistance commands? d. resource management of the system? e. resource usage accounting? f. security methods?				
2.	Is there Communications Software that allows interconnection with the necessary network architecture, such as: a. IBM - SNA, RJE, HASP, etc.? b. X.25 protocol? c. other?				
3.	Is there Data Management Software at the level desired, such as: a. file management b. DBMS? c. CODASYL compliant system?				
4.	Is Transaction Processing facilitated with: a. design and development aids? b. integration with COBOL, PL/1, etc.? c. key to disk/tape software? d. security features? e. backup and recovery features?				
5.	Is there an Applications Development language that is: a. compatible with your organization's standards? b. interactive?				

OPERATING SOFTWARE

No.	Item	Response			
		Yes	No	N/A	Comments
6.	Are there Productivity Aids available, such as: a. program report generators? b. screen handling and formatting methods? c. file information retrieval? d. database inquiry? e. interactive business graphics? f. Word Processing programs for documentation?				
7.	Are General Utility Programs available, such as: a. heading and dating programs? b. conversions? c. dollar sign and decimal handling? d. operations inquiries? e. page formatting and scrolling? f. other?				

in cooperation with the users, and should be used to confirm that the original application objectives were met. The test plan must fit the standards set by the Quality Assurance group, and exercise data under three conditions:

1. normal operations and normal flow of data;

2. the input of invalid data, either purposely or by error; and

3. the system behavior under abnormal conditions, such as hardware error, lack of required files, wrong timing of the updating, and so on.

The development of an adequate test plan is essential. There can easily be too much testing in unimportant areas, and full testing not achieved. Only with a plan can a high degree of reliability be obtained from testing in a reasonable amount of time.

Testing should not start "top down." At the gross system level, it is relatively easy for data to pass through the system correctly without exercising the greatest percentage of logical variables. Testing must start "bottom up" so that statements, algorithms, and programs can be tested and exercised individually before they are linked with other parts of the system.

The first application software tests should be by visual checking. The material and the programs must be read to determine their conformity to standards and the adequacy of the controls that are embedded in the system. The bulk of the testing should then be run with the test data. As many combinations and possibilities as possible should be exercised. Problems such as the improper closing of files, abnormal termination of a job by the computer operator, and the simultaneous attempt by two users to access identical data using an on-line program, should be simulated as well as possible, and the action of the software observed. In normal testing, the running of correct data to yield expected results should take the least time. Most energy should be put into trying to defeat the system or cause it to crash from a terminal.

Parallel tests are most helpful if they are feasible. Many small computer systems are designed to take advantage of new methods and more efficient equipment and approaches, however, and it is almost impossible to run parallel tests. The change in the operating procedures is too great.

Figure 5-2, Application Software - Evaluation and Testing, is a checklist to help review the completeness and effectiveness of the test plans and procedures. The final purpose of testing is to answer management's questions as to whether the acceptance criteria are met, and whether the application software is functioning as expected.

5.3 APPLICATION SOFTWARE - IMPLEMENTATION AND ACCEPTANCE

An application software system should never be implemented in the user's environment until it has been thoroughly tested and shaken out in the data processing environment by systems analysts, programmers, and other technical personnel. As was pointed out, testing can only be properly accomplished "bottom up," and the final testing in the user's area should be the topmost, or the last, of the tests. Only after the system has been thoroughly shaken out and run in practical conditions, preferably for several days, should full implementation be attempted.

Figure 5-2
(Page 1)

APPLICATION SOFTWARE - EVALUATION AND TESTING

No.	Item	Response			
		Yes	No	N/A	Comments
1.	Has an adequate test plan been developed for the application software to ascertain its integrity and reliability?				
2.	Does this test plan fit the standards for quality assurance in your organization?				
3.	Does this test plan handle the checking of performance under: a. normal operation? b. input of invalid data? c. unusual or abnormal situations?				
4.	Was a sufficient set of test data prepared by the systems analysts at the time of the functional requirements definition or the general systems design?				
5.	Are these test data still valid?				
6.	Are the tests developed from a "bottom up" direction at the following levels, depending upon the size of the system under test: a. coding of statements? b. accuracy of algorithm? c. program logic? d. syntax of job steps? e. assembly of jobstreams? f. requirements of the application? g. requirements of the system?				
7.	In the coding of the statements: a. Is there compliance with organization standards? b. Is there appropriate usage of the language? c. Are there sufficient comments?				
8.	In the accuracy of the algorithm: a. Is the logic correct? b. Is there compliance with organization standards? c. Have all complex algorithms been tested as subroutines?				

Figure 5-2
(Page 2)

APPLICATION SOFTWARE - EVALUATION AND TESTING

No.	Item	Response			
		Yes	No	N/A	Comments
9.	In the program logic: a. Is the logic flow straightforward and comprehensible? b. Does the logic meet the user requirements? c. Can the logic be charted readily? d. Is the program readable?				
10.	In the requirements of the application: a. Do all inputs, files, and outputs of the application meet the requirements requested by the user and noted in the functional requirements definition? b. Is a sufficient audit trail established? c. Are the controls workable and sufficient?				
11.	In the requirements of the system: a. Are all functions performing according to the specifications? b. Does the operation of the system on the computer meet performance expectations? c. Does the response and turnaround time at the terminals meet performance expectations? d. Do the output reports meet the user requirements? e. Are there adequate and sufficient controls on the system?				
12.	Have all phases of the application system been checked visually by appropriate technical personnel to review for readability, appropriate usage, and conformance to standards?				
13.	Have all parts of the system been run with the test data supplied by the system analyst?				
14.	Have parallel tests been scheduled wherever it is possible and reasonable to do so?				
15.	Has a report been prepared describing the tests applied, the test data used, and the results?				
16.	Have all the documentation and test reports been given to the organization's Quality Assurance group?				

System implementation must be a cooperative effort with the computer operations personnel working closely with the user personnel. Adequate training and agreement with the timing are essential. The users must be thoroughly trained in data handling, and the operating personnel must have prepared all files and controls. The implementation and cutover of the system can then be handled with everyone concerned watching the results.

Acceptance standards should have been defined in the system design and should be well-documented, if they are internal departmental procedures. At the time of acceptance, it is normal to refer back to the original functional requirements definition and user requirements to see if they have been met. The vendor will only be responsible for the computer acceptance criteria listed in the contract, but information services will be responsible to have an application system up and running that performs the functions that are required by the user.

Figure 5-3, Application Software - Implementation and Acceptance, is a checklist to review whether the necessary elements of the system are in place, and whether the acceptance standards have been met. The concern for security and disaster backup should also be covered at this time. This checklist merely points out the areas that should be covered. In actual practice, there will be many more questions to ask and points which will need review. These will have been developed individually for the system in its design and modification.

- **Application Software: System Maintenance:**

The approach to application software system maintenance will naturally vary depending upon the source of the software.

Internally-Developed Application Systems:

The users of small computer systems will normally have insufficient staff to handle any but the simplest system maintenance. They will depend upon the organization's central Technical Support group, or upon contract personnel. In any case, the problem of system maintenance will certainly arise, and it is preferable to have considered it in advance, and to have agreed on how it will be handled. Responsibility must be assigned before the fact.

Purchased or Leased Application Systems:

The application system maintenance support to be expected of the vendor will vary considerably between vendors. Frequently, the purchaser pays little attention to the system maintenance clauses in the contract because the system requirements are so much more important. Reliable maintenance support is of great help in getting the system operational, however, and in keeping it running smoothly.

Hardware vendors tend to give more varied maintenance support and will get technical personnel on-site more quickly than those who just market software. This is because, when a problem arises, it is seldom completely clear whether it is a hardware problem or a software problem, and the hardware vendor wants to keep the equipment in place and running.

The most effective routine maintenance tool is the "hot line" service, where the vendor has people at the phones day and night to accept calls and direct them to people who can respond. "Hot line" handlers are frequently quite adept at answering calls and giving reasonably good response rapidly because they get so many similar calls about problems related to misunderstandings about the workings of the system. The true measure of a "hot line" service is whether, when a major problem arises, they direct it rapidly to technical personnel who can work on it.

When unusual or major difficulties occur, one of the best methods of handling it is the system dump to be examined. No vendor can be expected to have persons knowledgeable enough to examine system dumps except at their central or developmental office. Thus, a common practice among vendors is to:

- First, try to respond over the telephone.

- Second, have a system dump sent to their office for examination.

- Third, get technical people on-site to examine the situation.

Vendors should not be expected to have technical people sent rapidly to a site before the other avenues are exhausted unless the application is very large and critical to the user.

Figure 5-3, Application Software - Implementation and Acceptance, reviews the terms of implementation and acceptance.

Control of Maintenance and Modifications:

Whether the application system maintenance is handled internally or by vendors, it should be carefully controlled, with records kept of all actions taken. Copies of previous versions of application programs should always be kept safely until it has been shown that the present version is completely usable, and there are no files in existence that require the previous version.

Figure 5-4, Application Software - System Maintenance, is a checklist that covers these various considerations. It is worth reviewing all of these points well before system implementation. These are the key points regarding maintenance about which managers should be concerned.

Figure 5-3
(Page 1)

APPLICATION SOFTWARE - IMPLEMENTATION AND ACCEPTANCE

No.	Item	Response			
		Yes	No	N/A	Comments
1.	Have all planned testing of the programs, jobstreams, and application systems been completed?				
2.	Has all pre-implementation training been completed for:				
	a. terminal operators?				
	b. data control clerks?				
	c. user supervisors?				
3.	Has the system been tested completely and satisfactorily as a whole?				
4.	Has the user management been completely apprised of the state and timing of the implementation?				
5.	Are all necessary terminals and required hardware units in place?				
6.	Has sufficient documentation been distributed to all concerned?				
7.	Have all communications lines been installed and tested?				
8.	Has a detailed implementation plan been developed and approved?				
9.	Do all transactions have entries in the transaction dictionary or its equivalent?				
10.	Have all data elements been entered in the data dictionary with appropriate approval and control?				
11.	Have all modules been running at least two weeks without abnormal endings?				
12.	Have all operations procedures been written and approved?				

APPLICATION SOFTWARE - IMPLEMENTATION AND ACCEPTANCE

No.	Item	Response: Yes	No	N/A	Comments
13.	Has all documentation required by organization standards been approved by Quality Assurance (or its equivalent) and reviewed by Technical Support (or its equivalent)?				
14.	Have all controls been accepted by Internal Audit?				
15.	Have the following acceptance standards been met:				
	a. compliance with all acceptance procedures?				
	b. review of the functional requirements definition and its approval?				
	c. review of the general system design and its approval?				
	d. review of the detail system design and its approval?				
	e. review of the program documentation?				
	f. review of the application controls?				
	g. review of the operations procedures and documentation?				
16.	Has the Quality Assurance group (or its equivalent) checked all procedures they deem necessary to check?				
17.	Has Internal Audit made all analyses they deem necessary to make?				
18.	Is the user prepared to review the acceptance criteria that were agreed upon earlier and decide on acceptance?				
19.	Have the system's security measures been reviewed?				
20.	Are the system's security measures adequate?				
21.	Have detailed backup and recovery plans been made for the system?				
22.	Are the available backup and recovery capabilities adequate?				

Figure 5-4
(Page 1)

APPLICATION SOFTWARE - SYSTEM MAINTENANCE

No.	Item	Response			
		Yes	No	N/A	Comments
	Internally-Developed Application Systems				
1.	Has the responsibility been assigned for maintenance of the application system?				
2.	Is there an understanding of what will be agreed upon as the difference between system maintenance and system modification?				
3.	Is there an understanding that:				
	a. critical maintenance problems will be handled promptly?				
	b. other maintenance jobs will be handled on a priority basis?				
4.	Will critical maintenance work be started on a verbal request?				
5.	Is there an agreed form or memo to request other maintenance jobs?				
6.	Will there be adequate technical staff available to handle the ongoing maintenance of the system?				
	Purchased or Leased Application Systems				
7.	Is the level of maintenance support provided in the vendor contract for the application system:				
	a. telephone support, examination of system dumps and listings, on-site remedial services, and on-site consultant services?				
	b. telephone support, examination of system dumps and listings, and on-site remedial services available?				
	c. telephone support and examination of system dumps and listings only?				
	d. telephone support only?				
8.	Is the telephone support a "hot line" service that is available at all hours and days you may need it?				

APPLICATION SOFTWARE - SYSTEM MAINTENANCE

<table>
<tr><th rowspan="2">No.</th><th rowspan="2">Item</th><th colspan="4">Response</th></tr>
<tr><th>Yes</th><th>No</th><th>N/A</th><th>Comments</th></tr>
<tr><td></td><td><u>Purchased or Leased Application Systems (Continued)</u></td><td></td><td></td><td></td><td></td></tr>
<tr><td>9.</td><td>Does the vendor send out regular notifications of:
a. error corrections?
b. modifications to the package?
c. field reports of problems and solutions?
d. useful tips and user comments?</td><td></td><td></td><td></td><td></td></tr>
<tr><td>10.</td><td>Is a single group or person in your organization given sole responsibility for:
a. telephone contacts with the vendor?
b. discussion of errors, system dumps, and listings with the vendor?
c. acting as liaison with the vendor on-site?
d. receiving and handling modifications and field reports?
e. attending user group meetings and acting as liaison with other users?
f. planning and managing training session reservations?</td><td></td><td></td><td></td><td></td></tr>
<tr><td>11.</td><td>Is a single person in your organization responsible for understanding and controlling the formal maintenance agreement?</td><td></td><td></td><td></td><td></td></tr>
<tr><td>12.</td><td>Are new releases and major modifications of the package promised from the vendor on a scheduled basis?</td><td></td><td></td><td></td><td></td></tr>
<tr><td>13.</td><td>Is the warranty period of the package clearly understood by all affected groups in your organization?</td><td></td><td></td><td></td><td></td></tr>
<tr><td>14.</td><td>Has a plan been developed to review all possible problem areas with the package before the warranty period runs out?</td><td></td><td></td><td></td><td></td></tr>
<tr><td>15.</td><td>After your technical personnel have studied the system in detail, have they had an opportunity to request more system support from the vendor if it appears to be needed?</td><td></td><td></td><td></td><td></td></tr>
</table>

APPLICATION SOFTWARE - SYSTEM MAINTENANCE

No.	Item	Response			
		Yes	No	N/A	Comments
	<u>Control of Maintenance and Modifications</u>				
16.	Is there a written procedure for handling program changes, including authorization, verification, and documentation for audit trail?				
17.	Are the system compiler and utilities used for source program changes only under supervision and control?				
18.	Are copies of versions of programs transferred to diskette or cassette for storage under management control?				
19.	Is there a change file maintained for each application, with explanations entered for each change?				
20.	Is adequate testing performed on changes, including the running of several test cycles?				

5.4 APPLICATION SOFTWARE - QUALITY ASSURANCE

The checklist on Quality Assurance reviews a function which should be handled at the time of system implementation. Someone should have the responsibility of determining whether:

- all necessary documentation is available;
- all applicable standards and procedures have been adhered to;
- reports have been issued at the completion of the key development and installation phases; and
- the resultant system is of the quality expected by the user.

Some organizations have Quality Assurance groups or Quality Control groups. It is their function to continuously review adherence to standards and procedures and the meeting of specifications. They may also be interested in the measures of performance of the application system. The type of detailed review that must be done for quality assurance necessitates having many knowledgeable people at all phases of the system development and installation. In fact, the work that needs to be done is so detailed that one cannot expect it to be handled by a fairly small group. For this reason, many organizations appoint a small Quality Assurance group to merely act as coordinators and recorders. They certainly must be knowledgeable, but their function becomes to:

- state what quality assurance review must be carried out;
- organize people in the various information services functions to handle the quality assurance for their functions;
- follow up to assure that the quality assurance reviews are conducted; and
- report on the results of the quality assurance reviews.

Figure 5-5, Application Software - Quality Assurance, is a checklist that outlines many of the areas and questions that are of concern to the persons handling Quality Assurance of the application software being implemented.

5.5 APPLICATION SOFTWARE - DOCUMENTATION

Documentation is not one of the earlier considerations in the selection or development of application software, but it becomes of prime importance in the installation and acceptance phase. The installation of application software without complete, accurate, up-to-date documentation at all levels can cause considerable difficulty in the operations and maintenance phases of the system. It is better to get complete and adequate documentation prepared before the system has been finally accepted and used, than it is when problems arise at a later date.

Figure 5-5

APPLICATION SOFTWARE - QUALITY ASSURANCE

No.	Item	Response			
		Yes	No	N/A	Comments
	NOTE: This checklist is for Quality Assurance, Quality Control , or equivalent group.				
1.	Is all the necessary documentation available for:				
	a. functional requirements definition?				
	b. system design and specifications?				
	c. detail system design and coding?				
	d. input/output media, handling, and controls?				
	e. control specifications?				
	f. database and file specifications?				
	g. audit trail?				
	h. adherence to internal standards?				
	i. operations documentation, methods, and control?				
	j. performance standards expected to be achieved?				
	k. defined backup and recovery procedures?				
	l. adequate security procedures?				
	m. adherence to the conversion and implementation plan?				
	n. adherence to the testing plan and schedule?				
	o. satisfactory documentation of the testing results?				
	p. proper recording of development and installation costs?				
	q. satisfactory training of all involved?				
	r. meeting the specified acceptance criteria?				
	s. satisfaction of the user in the implementation?				
2.	Has the Quality Assurance function been involved in all phases of the package definition, selection, acquisition, and installation?				
3.	Have all applicable standards and procedures been adhered to?				
4.	Has Quality Assurance issued reports at the key development and installation phase completions?				

APPLICATION SOFTWARE - DOCUMENTATION

No.	Item	Response			
		Yes	No	N/A	Comments
1.	Does the prepared documentation package conform to the existing documentation standards of your organization?				
2.	If the vendor's documentation does not conform to your standards, have plans been accepted to modify it?				
3.	Does the terminal operator documentation have: a. clear representation of the screens? b. straightforward and clear text? c. complete list of error messages? d. details of data control information to be entered? e. information on getting help when needed?				
4.	Has the terminal operator documentation been tested by an experienced operator?				
5.	Have training classes been scheduled for all terminal operators using the documentation as training material?				
6.	Have controls been installed on the distribution of the documentation and its periodic revision?				
7.	Has responsibility been assigned to update the documentation when the package is revised or modified?				
8.	Is the documentation well-packaged so that it is obvious if a set is complete?				
9.	Is there a revision control sheet attached to the documentation copies?				

As much of the documentation as possible should have been reviewed before the selection of the package.

Figure 5-6, Application Software - Documentation, is a checklist to help review the adequacy of the material before the system is accepted. The main points are:

- Does the documentation conform to your standards?
- Is there sufficient documentation for the terminal operator, and has it been tested before acceptance?
- Is the documentation adequate as training or self-study material?
- Are all sets of the documentation, and their revisions, under control?

• **<u>Application Software - Training Requirements:</u>**

New application software nearly always introduces new methods and procedures. At the least, the controls will be different from those previously used, and the naming of the variables, data, and reports will be new to the clerical and user professional personnel. More likely, there will be whole new concepts introduced of on-line, real-time operation. Personnel will have to radically change their mode of operation and use CRT tubes or other input devices instead of pen and paper. The many problems inherent in such a change must be thought about in advance, with their solutions incorporated in planned training programs.

Some personnel will take a positive view and think of the new opportunities opening up and the chance to learn the up-to-date methods. Many other personnel will initially be quite wary and have real concerns about the effects on their environment, their job activities, and even their jobs themselves. Such normal and reasonable concerns must be met with answers in a training environment.

Figure 5-20, Application Software - Training Requirements, is a checklist to help review the status of the training that has been received, or is planned, for all levels of personnel in your organization. Before the implementation is attempted, all training classes should be reviewed, a training program should be firmed up for at least a year, and all interested personnel should be offered the opportunity to participate in specific training sessions.

APPLICATION SOFTWARE - TRAINING REQUIREMENTS

No.	Item	Response: Yes	No	N/A	Comments
1.	Have the following received appropriate training for full operation of the application system: a. user management? b. user technical personnel? c. user supervisors? d. data control clerks? e. terminal operators? f. computer operators? g. systems programmers? h. systems analysts? i. internal audit personnel? j. quality assurance personnel?				
2.	Are sufficient training materials on hand for six months of start-up and operation?				
3.	Have necessary training classes been planned for the next year?				
4.	Has the equipment vendor supplied the system training outlined in the contract?				
5.	Are training materials on the system, such as manuals and audio-visuals, available in the Information Services library?				
6.	Have all concerned technical personnel been alerted to the existence of the system, and given an opportunity to receive training in it, or appropriate training materials?				
7.	Have the organization's training personnel had an opportunity to comment on the training materials?				

SECTION 6

OPERATIONS CONSIDERATIONS

SECTION OVERVIEW

The computer operations controls and procedures should be planned in advance and installed as the system is implemented. Specific instructions must be given to the operators as to the policies and procedures to follow and the forms to be used routinely. If the staff is small and there are recurrent changes in demands and schedules, it is normal for the operations to become informal with consequent loss of control. This tendency can be guarded against by documenting schedule changes, insisting that the operator follow procedures, and maintaining routine and consistent supervision of the operation.

Most operator actions in areas such as data handling and control, scheduling, equipment care, problem or incident reporting, and output production and distribution, may be followed by the supervisor by having the operator routinely fill out form sheets or control sheets. Most of the items on the following checklists are adaptable to objective, written reports if it is considered that they should be used regularly:

Figure 6-1: Computer Operations Control

Figure 6-2: Operations Procedures and Policies

Most equipment vendors will supply a variety of operation control form sheets to help observe the operational experience, to report problems or incidents, and to keep a record of the response and actions of their service personnel. The following control sheets are provided for this purpose:

Figure 6-3: Equipment Care Checklists

Figure 6-4: Equipment Care Log

Figure 6-5: Problem or Incident Reports

6.1 COMPUTER OPERATIONS CONTROL

Even a small computer system operation can be considered as a production line or "factory" which is accepting raw material and turning out products on set schedules. No system should ever be operated on pressure, demand, or "whim." It should be operated with set objectives and responsibilities, routine procedures to be followed, and regular reports to be produced. Adequate controls must be in place and must be monitored. Basic production statistics should be gathered in a form that is of interest to management.

Figure 6-1, Computer Operations Control, is a checklist that outlines the areas of monitoring, control, and logging which should be considered.

6.2 OPERATIONS PROCEDURES AND POLICIES

In the operations area, there is little difference between the direct controls that are in place and the procedures that must be followed to maintain a smooth and controlled operation. Procedures and policies must be translated to logs, schedules, and priorities, and handled objectively. The procedures followed by the operators produce the data for management control and quality assurance studies.

Figure 6-2, Operations Procedures and Policies, is a checklist to review items that should fall under operational policy and be handled as routine procedures. Among the procedures mentioned are those taken to assure the necessary security and privacy of the operation, and for the preparations for possible disaster recovery.

6.3 OPERATION CONTROL FORM SHEETS

All the procedures in this section should be handled on form sheets which are relatively simple to use by the operator. Nearly all scheduling, operations, and control actions can be described quickly on a form sheet. As many as possible of the actions should, of course, be handled automatically by the operating system being used, or by other utility routines that have been prepared. Many actions, however, are readily handled manually by the operator, and the form can be easily distributed to interested supervision.

Figure 6-3, Equipment Care, is the type of form that an equipment manufacturer will normally supply. It is most helpful to remind an operator, each shift, which equipment care actions should be taken. It will be changed only occasionally. It also aids the supervisor, when combined with **Figure 6-4, Equipment Care Log,** to review what care should have been taken and what was accomplished.

Figure 6-5, Problem or Incident Report, is an important audit trail of problems and the way they were handled. It is sometimes called a Trouble Report. Any form that is desired may be set up by management, but the vendor service personnel will probably only fill out and sign their particular, authorized reports. Misunderstanding can arise from reports that appear to indicate the service person did not perform as was expected. The usual solution is to use the vendor's Problem Report and append to it any internal reporting that may be helpful to your management.

Figure 6-1
(Page 1)

COMPUTER OPERATIONS CONTROL

No.	Item	Response			
		Yes	No	N/A	Comments
1.	Does the computer operation report to a single manager who handles scheduling and priority problems and future planning?				
2.	Has the computer operations group been given a written set of objectives and responsibilities?				
3.	Can the computer operations group reject a system that does not fit the accepted operating conditions?				
4.	Has the computer power supply been monitored for fluctuations and "spikes" that may disrupt the computer processing?				
5.	Have the ambient humidity, temperature, and dust conditions been studied, with appropriate controls applied?				
6.	Have the possibilities of harmful static electricity been studied and appropriate measures taken to prevent it?				
7.	Are adequate fire and water detection and control methods in place?				
8.	In the event of equipment malfunction, are there provisions for rapid repair or replacement?				
9.	Does the operator run diagnostic test programs regularly?				
10.	Is peak-volume activity, transaction growth, and regular usage of the system monitored regularly with an analysis made of the present and projected work compared to the level of capacity of the system?				
11.	Does the vendor give rapid aid in the event of operating system problems?				
12.	Is someone in internal Technical Support assigned to respond promptly in the event of software problems?				

COMPUTER OPERATIONS CONTROL

No.	Item	Response			
		Yes	No	N/A	Comments
13.	Are there adequate input data controls to prevent data loss, destruction, or manipulation?				
14.	Is there adequate operating system and application system documentation for routine operations?				
15.	Are problem or incident reports prepared promptly by the computer operator and studied by management?				
16.	Is the system activity logged and monitored automatically?				
17.	If there is no automated logging feature, is a manual log maintained?				
18.	Does management periodically review the system logs?				
19.	Are there procedures and controls for distributing output, and for storing printouts, diskettes, tapes, etc.?				
20.	Are basic operating statistics produced routinely, including:				
	a. job throughput and schedule adherence?				
	b. job turnaround time?				
	c. problems or incidents?				
	d. resource utilization?				

Figure 6-2
(Page 1)

OPERATIONS PROCEDURES AND POLICIES

No.	Item	Response			
		Yes	No	N/A	Comments
1.	Has the workflow through the computer been analyzed and established, including: a. data preparation? b. job setup and input? c. priorities of execution? d. output handling?				
2.	Has the impact of the system on the surrounding operations been evaluated?				
3.	Has the computer scheduling function been assigned to the computer supervisor as an ongoing area to be handled?				
4.	Is a regular job production schedule normally used?				
5.	Are management guidelines available to assist in the scheduling?				
6.	Does the scheduling supervisor plan at least a month in advance?				
7.	Are the priorities and schedules reviewed with all the users?				
8.	Are schedules kept flexible to adjust for special runs requested by management?				
9.	Have highly critical production jobs and their processing schedules been identified to the operations group?				
10.	Is there a system for assigning program priorities?				
11.	Is there some flexibility allowed in receiving critical user input?				
12.	Is the incoming work checked to verify that all input material to be processed is present?				
13.	Is there a written procedure indicating the course of action of all the work not present?				

OPERATIONS PROCEDURES AND POLICIES

No.	Item	Response: Yes	No	N/A	Comments
14.	Are all jobs logged on receipt, either by hand or automatically?				
15.	Are controlled operational programs processed only by the assigned operator?				
16.	Does the computer operator follow standard, formal procedures:				
	a. when the hardware fails?				
	b. for abnormal termination of production problems?				
17.	Are there written procedures for bursting, decollating, and distributing output reports?				
18.	Is a log maintained of diskette, disk, or tape activity and problems?				
19.	Is a log maintained to measure computer performance continuously, to evaluate the operations?				
20.	When a new system is contemplated, is the impact on the available resources and schedules evaluated?				
	<u>**Security and Privacy**</u> (See Section 11)				
21.	Are adequate security procedures in place?				
22.	Have privacy considerations been reviewed?				
23.	Has the insurance on the system been reviewed?				
24.	Have all vital records been selected, documented, and controlled?				
25.	Have adequate fire precautions been taken?				
26.	Has the security of the library and files been studied and controlled?				
27.	Have problems of personnel security been addressed?				

OPERATIONS PROCEDURES AND POLICIES

No.	Item	Response			
		Yes	No	N/A	Comments
	Disaster Recovery and Backup (See Section 12)				
28.	Have contingency plans been formalized for response to trouble?				
29.	Are copies of data, programs, and system procedures kept in a secure, separate location?				
30.	Have formal agreements for backup been made with other organizations?				
31.	Does the backup facility itself offer satisfactory security?				
32.	Has a system recovery plan been developed with each step assigned to an employee?				
33.	Has a disaster ever been simulated, with the backup facility used, as a rehearsal?				

Figure 6-3

EQUIPMENT CARE

Equipment Item	Care Applicable To This Item	Frequency of Care			Notes
		Daily	Weekly	Monthly	

Figure 6-4

EQUIPMENT CARE LOG

Computer System ____________________

Serial No. ____________________ Year __________

Item or Device ____________________ Page __________

Care Action	Record Date (Month/Day) each time a "care action" is performed

PROBLEM OR INCIDENT REPORT

Computer System	Serial No.	Location
Item or Device		

Problem Symptoms

	Date	Time	Operator
Problem First Occurred			
Vendor Called			
Service Person Arrived			
Service Completed			

Problem Diagnosis (Vendor Service)

Action Taken

Follow-up Necessary

Vendor Service: ______________

Operator ______________

Reviewed By: ______________

REVIEWING THE OPERATION OF SMALL COMPUTER SYSTEMS

SECTION 7

RELATED REFERENCES

(Selected by permission from "Quarterly Bibliography of Computers and Data Processing," Applied Computer Research, P.O. Box 9280, Phoenix, Arizona.)

BOOKS AND REPORTS

Auditing Computer Systems. FTP, 1978- Variable paging 4 Vols. $495.00.

A loose-leaf reference service providing information necessary to establish the EDP audit function, to outline the necessary tools, techniques, and approaches for use in auditing, and to suggest methodologies for management to evaluate the EDP audit function. Covers audit of applications, system design efforts, and computer centers with heavy emphasis on control practices. Updated semiannually.

PERIODICALS

Blank, H.I. **Criteria Necessary for Good Package Choice.** MIS WEEK 4:18, Jun 15, 83.

Advises users to consider the following in selecting software package function requirements, capacity requirements, software quality, and needs for transferability of data.

Brown, Nander Jr. **Minicomputers Control, Security, and Audit.** INT AUD 40:39-42, Feb 83.

Discusses audit and other issues for internal auditors' consideration in the review of a minicomputer installation.

Cimo, Guy. **Is Micro Migration Causing Database Mayhem?** COMPWRLD 17:SR 61+, MAR 28, 83.

Discusses problems with business use of microcomputers including insufficient storage capacity, inaccessibility to necessary information on mainframe files, and proliferation of data bases.

Dodge, John M. **Reckless Micro Acquisition Brings Trouble.** SOFT NEWS 2:28, DEC 82.

Describes the lack of planning regarding the acquisition and use of microcomputers and associated software in business, despite the speed with which micros are entering large companies.

Edwards, Chris. **Developing Microcomputer-Based Business Systems.** J SYS Mgmt 34:36-8, APR 83.

Addresses the different situation for developers of micro-based systems from that faced by developers of mainframe-based systems.

Evolution of Usage Creates Unique Problems. SOFT NEWS 2:20-1, OCT 4, 82.

Illustrates how the use of microcomputers, originally intended for limited use, can grow to cause unique situations.

Fogler, Robert A. **The Impact of the Microcomputer.** INT AUD 40:38-41, APR 83.

Contends that the best approach for an internal auditing department with limited resources is to obtain a microcomputer for exclusive use and to gain hands-on experience.

Foster, Susan. **Micro Departments May Be the Way.** COMP DEC 15:94+, JUN 83.

Describes the emergence of micro departments or managers to bridge the gap between MIS/DP departments and individual micro users in major companies.

Good, Phillip I. **Maintaining Your Micro - All Year.** COMP DEC 14:82+, DEC 82.

Suggests that users ensure that on-site maintenance is part of every sales contract for a personal computer and that they foster habits of preventive maintenance through checklists, posters, user manuals and training programs.

Holley, Charles L and Millar, Frederick. **Auditing the On-Line, Real-Time Computer System.** J SYS MGMT 34:14-9, JAN 83.

Discusses the complexity and risks involved in the on-line, real-time computer system, as well as such control issues as unauthorized access, audit trail considerations, and transmission errors. 18 references.

Krippaehne, Thomas M. **The Right Way To Select a Microcomputer.** DATA MGMT 20:26Z-DD, OCT 82.

Provides a method for determining and choosing the right microcomputer for individual needs.

Lebow, Max A. **Micros More Than Ready for Mainframe Shops.** COMPWRLD 17:SR 7+, MAR 28, 83.

Discusses programmer aids for microcomputers that range from symbolic assemblers and cross-reference utilities for higher level languages to full-blown application generators.

McCusker, Tom. **DPers Differ on Implementation of Micro Policies.** SOFT NEWS 2:4, DEC 82.

Discusses the proliferation of microcomptuers in businesses from the perspective of data processing personnel at banks throughout the U.S.

McMullen, Edwin G. **Some Advice for DP Managers on Micro Integration.** COMPWLRD 17:SR 3-4, MAR 28, 83.

Summarizes issues affecting the integration of micros into larger processing systems including equipment standardization, software transportability, data extraction, service support, and who will purchase the microcomputers.

Morley, Ann. **DBMS for Micros.** COMPWRLD OA 17:41-3+, JUN 15, 83.

Reviews data base management systems, machines and related networks for microcomputers.

Morley Pete. **Getting the Most for Your Money.** COMP DEC 14:74+, NOV 82.

Suggests some alternatives to consider when organizing microprocessing for an entire company.

Neibaur, Dale. **Micro Installation Requires Careful Planning.** COMPWRLD 17:SR 41-2, MAR 28, 83.

Contends that the effective use of two or more personal computers in a business environment requires that the computers share information easily and efficiently, which can be accomplished by a local-area network.

The Software Catalog: Minicomputers. Elsevier, 1983- $191.50/yr standing order.

A comprehensive, continuously updated reference service for information about the availability, price, applications, and compatibility of packaged software for minicomputers.

Trimmer, Dan. **Micro/Mini Migration - Don't Lose Control.** IBM USER p. 39+, SEP 82.

Evaluates minicomputers and microcomputers for the commercial user, with discussion of IBM's stance, capacity, communication links, and file handling.